The Blueprint of Grace

The Blueprint of Grace

Seeing and Submitting to God's Design for Sanctification

ROBERT ALLEN

Foreword by Chris Thomas

WIPF & STOCK · Eugene, Oregon

THE BLUEPRINT OF GRACE
Seeing and Submitting to God's Design for Sanctification

Copyright © 2024 Robert Allen. All rights reserved. Except for brief quotations in critical publications or reviews, no part of this book may be reproduced in any manner without prior written permission from the publisher. Write: Permissions, Wipf and Stock Publishers, 199 W. 8th Ave., Suite 3, Eugene, OR 97401.

Wipf & Stock
An Imprint of Wipf and Stock Publishers
199 W. 8th Ave., Suite 3
Eugene, OR 97401

www.wipfandstock.com

PAPERBACK ISBN: 978-1-6667-8904-1
HARDCOVER ISBN: 978-1-6667-8905-8
EBOOK ISBN: 978-1-6667-8906-5

VERSION NUMBER 02/29/24

Scripture quotations are from the English Standard Version, copyright © 2001 Crossway, a publishing ministry of Good News Publishers. Used by permission. All rights reserved.

Scripture quotations marked CSB have been taken from the Christian Standard Bible, copyright © 2017 by Holman Bible Publishers. Used by permission. Christian Standard Bible® and CSB® are federally registered trademarks of Holman Bible Publishers.

For you who wrestle with God's plan for your life

Contents

Foreword | ix
Acknowledgements | xiii
Introduction | xvii

1 God's Plan in Creation | 1
2 God's Plan for Mankind | 11
3 God's Plan through Jesus | 22
4 God's Plan through the Holy Spirit | 33

Interlude | 43

5 The Blueprint | 45
6 The First Steps of Faith | 51
7 Putting On the New: Growing in Obedience | 59
8 The Unexpected Uh-Ohs | 68
9 Building Up the Body (Part I): The Life of the Church | 75
10 Building Up the Body (Part II): The Ministry of the Church | 83
11 The Future Glory of the Church and You | 91

Conclusion: An Invitation | 95
Bibliography | 99

Foreword

THE EXCITEMENT EBBED AWAY with my first breath. Now, to be honest, I'm not an overly excitable guy; I'm fairly reserved in my displays of emotion. But I *had* been undeniably excited; that much was clear. But not anymore.

A week or two earlier, my wife and I had purchased an old van, circa late 1970s, that had been permanently parked on a slab of concrete wrapped in old corrugated iron, and had numerous little extensions tacked onto it over the last thirty years or so. Our intention was to make some small renovations, tidy it up, and use it as a beach house retreat for family holidays, and as a place for others in need of some Sabbath rest to have an inexpensive break away. The location is stunning. Nestled among the Australian bush landscape, overlooking a quiet stretch of water that winds its way out into the Pacific Ocean, sits our little shack. In my mind, the primary vision was wrapped in all the potential, the finished product, the place where I and others could rest. Of course, somewhere in the back of my consciousness was the annoying voice of the realist the dwells within. *You got a fair bit of work here, mate. It's not going to be easy.*

I'd say that my sense of expectation was most akin to the hopes and dreams of my youth—full of visions for how things *will* be, without giving much thought for the journey required to get there. I recall the zeal of my early twenties, the vision I'd constructed of my victorious Christian life, the ministries I'd have transformed, and maybe even built. I remember thinking about how much easier my Christian life would be when I was older, when I'd conquered youthful lusts, had overcome the temptations that assailed me, and looked more like Jesus than I did then. I guess I must have thought that with enough time, things would get better, as though the passing of years would, in and of itself, achieve something that I longed for.

But now, here I was looking at my beach house—the passing of time had not been kind. Of course, there was a kind of rustic charm, a weathered patina that told a story of the years that etched themselves into it—yet there was no mistaking it; more time was not the cure for what ails my crumbling little shack. It was at this point, as I breathed in the musty air that carried with it the smell of rotting timber and carpet that had never truly dried, that the annoying voice of the realist suddenly grew louder. *See? I told you this was going to be a lot of work!*

My wife and I sat on the edge of an old step and looked around us as our younger children excitedly rummaged through the ruins and laid claim to rooms and spaces as though they were turn-of-the-century explorers. "That bit looks good, honey; we won't have to do much in there," came my wife's optimistic voice. I nodded, but I was looking at everything else—my excitement was fast ebbing away. *I've been here before*, I thought.

And I had.

In my mid-forties, my faith was much like our beach house—full of potential, full of promise, full of what could be—but left dormant for too long, left to the buffeting effects of wind and rain, waiting out the scorching summers and unattended winters, my faith began to stink. I had foolishly thought that time would be the vehicle of sanctification, that being an *older* Christian would automatically make me a more *Christlike* Christian. But it hadn't. The veneer on my faith looked uncomfortably like the veneer on our shack—as I tore away the lining, ripped up the carpet, ferried trailer after trailer to the local tip, more and more structural damage was exposed. A *light makeover* has grown into a full-blown renovation.

Foreword

Covered in filth and sweat, I sat down for a cool glass of water that my wife poured for me, and said between sips, "It might have been easier to just knock the whole thing down and build something new."

"Maybe," she replied. "But this will be *better*."

I'd lost the vision for what this would be. All I could see was the labor involved—I was staring at the sunken foundation that needed reinforcing—but my wife was staring at the weekends we'd spend fishing with the kids, the families that would be blessed by the space we were creating. She was keeping her eyes open to the possibilities, even while her hands were dirty with the work required to achieve it. And in that moment, by an act of pure grace, Jesus stood beside my wife and knowingly nodded as she uttered those words.

Yes, there is much work needed during the hard years of sanctification—time alone is insufficient. But the work required, as back-breaking as it may be, isn't the sole answer either. The effort required by my own hand will fall far short, just as the passing of years do—because what I actually need is the transformative work of grace. It is the gospel that must tear away the veneer, rip up the mouldy carpets, relay the foundation, and resheet the roof. Yes, it will take time. Yes, it will take hard work and no small amount of sweat and tears. But it will happen, because Jesus has not lost sight of what he's doing in us, and he has not lost the resolve to achieve what he has begun.

> I am sure of this, that he who started a good work in you will carry it on to completion until the day of Christ Jesus. (Phil 1:6 CSB)

I made the thirty-minute drive out to the shack just the other day. I stepped through the front door and took a deep breath; I could smell the fresh aroma of new timber, of a freshly laid floor, and paint that had recently dried. I know that just in the other room there is still a small leak from a roof that needs attention, and there is more painting to be done, more walls to finish lining, and some lights that need rewiring. It's not done yet, but it soon will be.

Foreword

Now, on the off chance you have concluded that I am some sort of renovating wizard, let me assure you, I am far from it—I've had plenty of help along the way. I've enjoyed quite a few days of enjoyable fellowship with old friends who've shared their expertise and experience with me, who've sat in the dust with me, problem-solved with me, and left their mark on the finished product that I couldn't have accomplished on my own. My shack needed my friends—just like my faith has.

I've not met Bob in person yet; we live on seperate continents a world away from each other. I hope one day we might share a hot coffee together as we watch the sunrise over the water near my shack. But Bob *is* my friend, and a friend that has left his mark on the renovation of my faith. I'm glad for his wisdom, which I know has been gleaned at great cost and with deep heartache—the wise counsel he offers over the following pages will continue to guide the work that yet remains in my own walk of faith, and I'm sure you'll find it helpful as well.

I'm not done yet. But I soon will be.

You're not done yet. But the plan is there, and, by grace, you soon will be too.

—Chris Thomas
Teaching Pastor
Raymond Terrace Community Church

Acknowledgements

FIRST AND FOREMOST, I thank God for saving me, for loving me, for guiding me, for blessing me, and for helping me understand his character. I am a sinner redeemed by the blood of Jesus and I know it. I am eternally amazed and grateful for what God has wrought in my life. This whole project in some ways stems from my own quest to understand my life and faith. It has taken me years to wrap my head around God's abundant and unfailing grace and my hope is that this book helps you see it too.

This book would not exist without the church I grew up in and those who discipled me as a teenager. If you've read the book, you know that for good or ill I am what I am because of my upbringing in the church. There are any number of names I can point to along the way who have shaped me as a Christian: my mom and dad, Jim and Virginia Armstrong, Charlie Arsenault, John Wilson, Chuck Price, Jay and Cat Cleveland, Jason Mirikitani, Jeff Fox, Greg Thomas, Jeff Fabbiano, Mark Bellanger, David Stark, Matt Uhles, Mike and Jenny Lape, John O'Shaughnessy, Pat Gorsett, Patrick Ryan, Joe Nichols, Jeremy Payne, Paul List, Roger Vester, Ed Gregory, Chase Abner, Doug Rowland, and so on. There are too many names beyond these, so if I have left you out, my apologies. Every life that has crossed paths with mine over the years has left an imprint.

But when I stop and think about the seeds of this book and the soil it grew in, there are certain folks who come to mind. Back

Acknowledgements

in 2019, I found myself on the launch team for a fantastic look at the doctrines of grace titled *Humble Calvinism*, by Jeff Medders. Through that process, I found myself engaged with people around the globe, two of whom have been my biggest supporters through this process: Messers Alistair Chalmers and Chris Thomas. It was Alistair who first invited me to join a writing group headed up by Tim Challies, which eventually folded into the Gospel Centered Discipleship organization. It was in this writing group that I first encountered Chris. Both Alistair and Chris encouraged, shared, and pushed my writing. These two pastors have shaped my thoughts and heart more than they know and I am forever grateful for their investment in my life, ministry, and writing. They have been side-by-side with me along this journey, cheering me on and helping me clarify my thoughts throughout. This book would not exist without their prayers and support.

This manuscript came about because of Jeremy Writebol, the executive director of GCD. I sent him a message back in 2020 about whether or not the idea behind this book, illustrating the process of sanctification through the metaphor of home remodeling reality TV, was worth chasing down. He encouraged me to knock together a proposal and give it a whirl. He has been in my corner throughout, advising, rooting, and cajoling me when necessary. This wouldn't have seen the light of day without him.

I would be remiss if I didn't mention the Gospel Centered Discipleship Writers' Guild. This international group of folks who are dedicated to creating Christ-centered content warms my heart. There is a long list of folks here, so if I overlook you or your contribution, I am sorry. But I'd like to thank, in no particular order, Benjamin Vrbicek, Timarie Friesen, Adsum Ravenhill, Lara d'Entremont, Brianna Lambert, Ashley Anthony, Amy Hornbuckle, Heidi Kellogg, Andrea Sanborn, Jessica Trevena Miskelly, Nicholas Lewis, Ira Hall, Kris Sinclair, and Russ Meek.

Above all of these people, I want to thank my wife, Mandy. Through the writing of this book over the last couple of years, there have been setbacks and frustrations, which I have shared and vented onto the love of my life. She has been encouraging and

Acknowledgements

supportive even when I've gotten out of bed in the middle of the night to revise words, paragraphs, and chapters that didn't sit right with me. She has given me space to be excited and dejected. She has graciously given me time to dedicate to writing while she cares for our house and our children. She has truly been an unsung hero of my life and ministry. She is a gift from God, one that never fails to amaze or encourage me. Dearest Mandolin, thank you.

Introduction

THIS IS THE DAY I get found out.
This is the day people figure out that I'm not anything special.
This is the day when people see through my facade to who I really am.
There are probably days when these sentences, these thoughts, pass through your mind before your feet hit the floor in the morning. I know that to be true because it happens to me too.
And I'm a pastor.
I'm what you would consider a run-of-the-mill mid-forties male. I struggle with the things that you can imagine any run-of-the-mill mid-forties male struggles with, things like anger, pride, jealousy, lust, and so on. As such, being who I am and doing what I do has brought me to a pretty tense place.
I know who I am.
I know who God wants me to be.
I know I'm not who God wants me to be.
I know that the people of my church and my community think higher of me than I think of myself because I know I'm not who God wants me to be.
I've spent much of my adult life dealing with this reality, this gap between public persona and private self-realization. I grasp what the Bible says about being a Christian; what God has decreed and commanded does not escape me. I've dedicated several years of

Introduction

my life to understanding those truths more deeply, to incorporating them into my life, and to teaching others to do the same.

It's why I wrote this book—for me and, by proxy, for you.

I had spent nearly two decades following God, trying to stay on the path God laid out for me, but I tripped, stumbled, and fell through life as I tried to outrun my laziness, my sexual appetites, and my insecurities. Then one day, God began a work in my heart shortly before my baptism in 2010. It happened this way.

As I was reading my Bible, I happened across Philippians 3, where Paul is describing his old pharisaical life and its comparison to his new one. I was confused by what I read. It sounds like Paul was doing the right things at the time, right? "If anyone else thinks he has reason for confidence in the flesh, I have more: circumcised on the eighth day, of the people of Israel, of the tribe of Benjamin, a Hebrew of Hebrews; as to the law, a Pharisee; as to zeal, a persecutor of the church; as to righteousness under the law, blameless" (Phil 3:4-6). I had enough sense to see that Paul was explaining his pre-conversion, but it began to eat away at me. I could understand that Paul had spent his whole life acting like one of God's people. He, like the rich young ruler (Matt 19:16-22), had followed the commandments to perfection. But once Jesus met Paul on the road to Damascus, all the doing became useless. "But whatever gain I had, I counted as loss for the sake of Christ. Indeed, I count everything as loss because of the surpassing worth of knowing Christ Jesus my Lord. For his sake I have suffered the loss of all things and count them as rubbish, in order that I may gain Christ" (Phil 3:7-8).

And there it was, in plain view for me to see. All of the moral things I had been striving to do, as good as they were, would never be what saved me. In fact, those good deeds were "rubbish." The Greek word is pretty crass actually: *skubalon*—dung. In Paul's eyes, knowing Jesus changed his opinion on how he had lived his entire life. It was quite the reversal. He had to not only give up confidence in his entire way of life; he now saw his former confidence as shame. To move forward, he had to dismantle his former identity.

When I realized being right with God wasn't a matter of me doing the right things but being in relationship with the right

Introduction

Person, suddenly, both my perspective on my behavior and my actual behavior began to change. I could now handle the gap between who I knew I was, a sinful and broken man with a heart desperate for purity and wholeness, and the "nice young man" everyone else saw when they looked at me. Now, I'm not going to sit here and tell you that I'm killing it or that I perfectly trust in what Jesus did for me at the cross, because those would both be lies. But I will tell you that I know I'm not who God wants me to be and that's OK because I'm not who I used to be either.

Several years back I was blessed to be asked to deliver a commencement speech to the senior class of Braymer High School in Braymer, Missouri (props to the class of 2014!) If you've ever had pleasure of such a speaking engagement, you know it is both exciting and daunting. What do you say to people whom you know and like whose world is about to change drastically? What advice do you give to children deemed by society to be ready to be grown-ups? What wisdom do you dispense to a captive audience on the cusp of one of the biggest transitions they will ever face? I chose to speak on the task that lay ahead of any kid sitting in any high school gym listening to any commencement speaker—becoming who you really are. Regardless of location, urban to rural, something changes when you graduate high school. You leave behind the past and take your first step into the rest of your life. At the heart of the address was a deep conviction that who you are today is only a version of yourself. You are constantly in transition from who you were to who you will become.

And that's what this book is about: how we leave behind who we have been in order to become who God wants us to be. The technical term is *sanctification*, the process of becoming conformed to the image of Christ, as Paul references in Romans 8:29: "For those whom he foreknew he also predestined to be conformed to the image of his Son." (Now, understand that we *could* get into all the deep conversation about predestination at this point, but that's not the aim of this work.) The main thrust of Paul's words here is that God has a plan for his people, but it is important to note that Paul is not urging Roman Christians to act more Christlike, but to

Introduction

become Christlike. One of the first books about being a Christian I read was Max Lucado's *Just Like Jesus*. The basic premise is that God meets you where you are, but doesn't want you to stay where you are. He wants you to become just like Jesus, hence the title. It was transformative in many ways, but first and foremost I began to understand that there was something more that God was calling me to. When I read about this Christlikeness that God wanted from and for me, it felt like the early days following my big growth spurt between sixth and seventh grade.

I grew six inches in a summer and my feet went from a size 8 to size 11.5. I was the same kid, but I looked different. My brain still functioned like I was 5'0" but my body was now 5'6". That summer in Little League, I had a terrible year because my brain hadn't adjusted to my new gangly arms and legs. Not only was it physically painful to grow that much over such a short period, but my body didn't agree with what I wanted it to do and that was mentally taxing. Eventually, everything caught up, but man it was awkward for a bit.

In the same way, as God was working this new understanding of what it means to be a Christian in my heart, I began to see myself as a work in progress, a person not just changing my clothes or posture or accent to ape someone else, but someone who was fundamentally different from who I was the day before. I realized there was a path laid out before me that had less to do with doing Christian things and more with leaving behind my old self, specifically my old ways of thinking, in order to become Christlike. It's a cliché, but I had to keep reminding myself that God wasn't finished with me yet, which allowed me to have a little grace for myself because what God was doing in me was both hard and time consuming. (I say "was," but he is, of course, still accomplishing his will in me even as you read these words.) That's why I wrote this book. It flows out of my experiences in becoming who God wants me to be. But my experience is not solely mine. It is yours as well if you desire it to be.

I don't claim to be an expert, but one thing I have learned is that this sanctification stuff can be a little daunting to understand.

Introduction

What you're about to read is my attempt to explain it in such a way as to help you become who God wants *you* to be. As much as I'd like to, I can't tell you exactly who God wants you to be in any tangible sense. What I can do, however, is explain what the Bible says about engaging in the process of figuring it out and share snippets gleaned from my own experiences. Hopefully you find value in these revealed truths as you pursue whatever it is that God has laid before you. My prayer is that you are encouraged and inspired to let biblical truth shape the path forward to transform your life into one that increasingly reflects God's glory.

So, in trying to get at the heart of sanctification, and how Christians become set apart for God's purposes, we must first start with some backstory, some brief explanation of how we got where we are at the moment. Such a pursuit leads us to examine why, which ultimately leads us to a who.

In part 1, we will look to Scripture to provide us with a framework to understand where we are in this ever-unfolding story of God. Each chapter delves into a character, specifically seeing how they drive the saga of history forward. Our path begins at the beginning of all things with God, the creative mind behind the universe, and his purpose and plan in creation—to make himself known (chapter 1). The progressive nature of time leads us down through the ages to see how human beings—me and you and everyone else—have failed to remain faithful for God's plan for us (chapter 2). As such, God, in his grace and mercy, provided one who would come and live the life he intended for us, Jesus (chapter 3). Through this Jesus' life, death, burial and resurrection, God saves people from their sins, bringing them back into right relationship with him and indwelling them with his Holy Spirit, who acts as guide and seal for a future spent with God (chapter 4).

After a brief interlude, I hope to build on what we've learned in part 1.

In part 2, we'll dig into more of the actual nuts and bolts of how sanctification progresses. First, we'll see that God gives us a blueprint for sanctification, conformity to Christ (chapter 5). The first step to becoming Christlike is to become less like your former

Introduction

self. In order to turn into a better representation of Jesus, you must first turn away from the sins of your past life (chapter 6). The process is just that—a process. While your relationship with God is restored through Christ, as one being conformed to Christlikeness, you bear some responsibility to pursue what God intends for you through intentional investment in your own spiritual life (chapter 7). Of course, when you begin growing in your faith, you will mess it up. You will come up against obstacles and hindrances like past sins and patterns of behavior that you must submit to the authority of God and from which you must repent and continue to repent in perpetuity. The Chrisitan life is marked by a spirit of continual repentance and renewal (chapter 8). Thankfully, you don't undertake this process alone. You have a community of faith whose job is to help stay the course and become the person God desires you to be (chapter 9). This community, called "the church," exists to fulfill God's plan to cover the earth with his glory (chapter 10). Of course, every journey, every story, every life has an end. The end for those who are in Christ Jesus is glorious beyond comparison (chapter 11).

After we look at the path to Christlikeness and the end of that path, I'll lay out for you some next steps you can take to allow God to begin to remodel your life into one that better reflects his glory.

As we walk through the journey of sanctification together, I hope you, the reader, grasp what it means to submit yourself to God as you begin to see his unfolding plan for your life, leaving the end results in his capable hands.

With that said, let me begin laying the foundation.

1

God's Plan in Creation

Praise the Lord! Praise the Lord from the heavens; praise him in the heights! Praise him, all his angels; praise him, all his hosts! Praise him, sun and moon, praise him, all you shining stars! Praise him, you highest heavens, and you waters above the heavens! Let them praise the name of the Lord! For he commanded and they were created.

—Psalm 148:1–5

Do you remember the first experiment you ever designed in middle school or high school science class? And I don't mean the kind of experiment that begins with the words, "I wonder what would happen if I mixed all these flavors of pop from this pop dispenser in one cup." I mean the kind where you have to make a hypothesis and then test the hypothesis and then make observations and then draw some conclusions from your data based your original hypothesis and then produce a report with all that information. I can remember mine. When I was a sophomore, we had to create an experiment and my lab partner and I chose to filter light through different colors of cellophane and see which produced the best growth in a lima bean. We constructed red, green, and blue booths for our beans; we also allowed for an unfiltered version. Over the course of a month, we watered and watched and waited to see what would happen.

If you know anything about biology, chemistry, and physics, the results should be predictable. The process that drives growth in plants, photosynthesis, relies on energy from light. Plants absorb light from the sun or other sources, which aids in the process of converting carbon dioxide and water into food. The key chemical component, chlorophyll, causes plants to appear green to the human eye because it reflects that particular wavelength of the visible spectrum. In the end, the bean under the green light grew the slowest because it was reflecting rather than absorbing the light. The experiment happened pretty much exactly how we thought it would, but the whole process left me with a deeper question.

Why?

And I don't mean why in the sense of questioning the validity of asking a tenth-grader to design a scientifically reproducible and valid experiment. A nagging sense of something profound sprouted in my conscious mind. Why do I know the color green? Why can I differentiate it from blue or red or even just plain white? My brain got foggy. It wasn't the science that befuddled me; the most accomplished scientists, professors, or experts in neurology can tell us how the mechanics of it all works. No, the haziness grew out of a deep-seated inquisitiveness to not just deconstruct existence to a scientific *how*, but to arrive at an existential *why*. Ultimately, science provides no real answer for the very existence of the processes that convert the millions of stimuli bombarding the senses, ignoring some and focusing on others, in order to make some sense of the world.

The naturalist explains it away as just part of the preservation process. The brain adapts and focuses on what it needs to survive, allowing us to block out certain unnecessary information in order to be attentive to things that matter. The human mind can only focus on so much at one time and, as such, to succeed, the nervous system's command center works like a strainer, letting what matters pass through and filtering what doesn't. But chasing that rabbit brings yet more questions. If it's all just a biological process, one that evolved over hundreds of thousands of years, as naturalists believe, why do we find sunsets beautiful? Why do certain vibrations of the air, the trill of a wren, the mournful tone of the cello, or the voice of our love stir our souls?

For the naturalist, there is nothing behind the scenes, only an unfolding system of science that randomly began billions of years ago with no real purpose for existing and will continue until it doesn't. If that's the case, we would have no reason to find beauty or heartache or joy, only chemical responses that reflexively push us to survival.

But we do find beauty, we do experience heartache, we do feel joy. It is a mystery, is it not? Human existence provokes the quest to look for something deeper than science, something more than mere equations and numbers to explain it. We wrestle with what happens in the day-to-day of life because of an elusive longing. But in all of the searching, people have come to neglect a simultaneously simple yet utterly beyond comprehension explanation—there is both a grand design and a grand Designer. Some might erroneously chalk it up to Occam's razor (the simplest answer is the most likely), but such a decision inaccurately applies Occam's principle and, more importantly, sells the majesty of creation short.

Since the beginning of recorded history, because the complexity of the universe cannot be trivialized nor dismissed, people have postulated and theorized about life on earth, fabricating for themselves systems of belief in their efforts to pinpoint significance in it. The question "Why am I here?" lies beneath every word ever written, and the answer is deceptively singular. Let me put forward that the answers to the deepest questions about the universe are neither scientific nor philosophical but spiritual in nature, and when we begin to view the search for solutions to the nature of existence as a primarily spiritual pursuit, we find answers rather than more questions.

The Blueprint of Grace

God revealed himself...

From the very first sentence, the Bible makes clear its central tenet. "In the beginning, God created the heavens and the earth" (Gen 1:1). The text gives the reader no backstory, description of the character of this God, or explanation of why. It simply states that a being, *Elohim* as the Hebrew text reads, created the heavens and the earth. And before we run too far down the track, the Hebrew for created, *bara*, paints the picture that prior to God creating there was nothing. So out of nothing, something appeared, and that something was made by God in a specific fashion.

> The earth was without form and void, and darkness was over the face of the deep. And the Spirit of God was hovering over the face of the waters. And God said, "Let there be light," and there was light. And God saw that the light was good. And God separated the light from the darkness. God called the light Day, and the darkness he called Night. And there was evening and there was morning, the first day. And God said, "Let there be an expanse in the midst of the waters, and let it separate the waters from the waters." And God made the expanse and separated the waters that were under the expanse from the waters that were above the expanse. And it was so. And God called the expanse Heaven. And there was evening and there was morning, the second day. And God said, "Let the waters under the heavens be gathered together into one place, and let the dry land appear." And it was so. God called the dry land Earth, and the waters that were gathered together he called Seas. And God saw that it was good. (Gen 1:2–10)

Given no rationale for the dynamic unfolding in creation, the Bible heralds a who that is responsible for the cosmos, a first Cause from whom all things originate, *Elohim*—God. Put as simply as possible, the Bible asserts that life as we know it exists because God wills it so. Many discredit such a thought as antiquated or fantastical, opting instead to interpret their experiences in an enigmatic system through scientific observations and exploration because mathematics and science have revealed so much about how the universe functions. In short, nonscientific solutions have been deemed not only insufficient, but also irrational. Yet, when left to extrapolate some semblance of understanding from the complexity of science and mathematics that we now understand, what could be dismissed once as fanciful and imaginative spiritualism or mythology crafted to explain natural phenomena points us to a less labyrinthine answer. A. W. Tozer writes, "Unfortunately, we have left nature and creation to the scientists who are trying to unravel the mystery of our universe. It is my opinion that nature should automatically lead us to God, who is described for us in the Word of God as the Creator."[1] Nature points to something beyond it by its very complexity and beauty. That something is a Someone who unmasks himself through the Bible. This is the claim of the Bible: that everything in this life finds its cause in God.

There are many ideas about what the Bible is and what it's about, from a book of moral teaching to the story of how Judaism began and became Christianity. According to a 2017 Gallup poll, 24 percent of American adults surveyed, fewer than one in four, believe that the Bible is the literal word of God, less than the percentage of the population that believes it to be a "a book of fables, legends, history and moral precepts recorded by man."[2] This same organization has been tracking this data since the mid-1970s, and 2017 was the first time "biblical literalism has not surpassed biblical skepticism."[3] The numbers demonstrate that fewer and fewer are turning to the Bible to resolve the mysteries science has yet to unravel. Yet, life as we know it requires a precision unlikely found by mere happenstance, thus making the Bible's claim of a universe brought into existence by a being who predates its creation a weightier proposition.

---

1. A. W. Tozer, *Delighting in God,* Minneapolis, (MN: Bethany House, a division of Baker Publishing Group, 2015), 183.

2. Lydia Saad, "Record Few Americans Believe Bible Is Literal Word of God," Gallup, Gallup, May 15, 2017, https://news.gallup.com/poll/210704/record-few-americans-believe-bible-literal-word-god.aspx.

3. Saad, "Record Few Americans Believe Bible Is Literal Word of God."

So, to explore and unpack life is to explore and unpack the question, "Who is this *Elohim*?"

God revealed himself because he wants to be known . . .

Behind the first few verses of the Bible lies a compelling truth—the Being responsible for everything that exists wants to be known. The *Elohim* of Genesis 1 elevates himself above all else from the outset, establishing and ordering existence: light and dark, night and day, earth and sky, land and sea. The Bible begins with a display of God's immeasurable power, a power that humanity can never achieve. For all of our innovations and experiments and efforts, we cannot separate light and dark with our speech or create a single atom from nothingness. We can barely smash one into subatomic particles. Have you seen the sheer size of the Large Hadron Collider? We can break down and analyze what is within, but we are incapable of constituting from without. And in that tension between what we can and can't do, the Bible proclaims, from its very first words, One whose capability far exceeds our machinations and imaginations. In doing so, it defines the gap between Creator and created.

We are rightly awed when we contemplate the mind behind the universe and should be equally awed as we recognize the implications of his self-revelation. Consider for a moment the two parallel tracks. A single Entity initiated and established the cosmos and astonishingly, this very same uber-powerful and overwhelmingly different Entity makes himself known. Creation is a testimony to God, but only a partial one. Think of it this way: we can know that other people exist by the imprint they leave behind. It's how archaeologists piece together ancient life. Their digs uncover fragments about the everyday lives of those who lived ages ago, but tell us nothing of personalities or beliefs.

I'm reminded of the first house my wife and I moved into when we got married. By the coarse black hairs, the pungent odor, the streaks and stains on the walls, and the chunks of kibble mingled with grease spatters beneath the stove, we realized that whatever else happened to be true of the previous owners, they apparently had dogs and loved them because they kept them in the house. That is just one detail we could observe about the previous owners. We didn't know much else about them. Actually, we didn't know anything else about them. They didn't tack a note to the door with the greeting, "To the next residents of this house . . . ," explaining how they lived or why they lived the way they lived. We were left with a physical manifestation of who they were, but if we wanted to understand them, we would have to either fill in the gaps by reverse engineering what the results of their life wrought or track them down. Too busy scrubbing and painting the walls, tearing out carpet, and scouring the hardwood floors underneath, we did neither.

In the same way we could glean something about the previous tenants by observing the condition of the house when we moved in, people in antiquity might have perceived and attempted to understand God by checking out his creation. The cosmos does provide an archaeological record, tangible, observable, and decipherable, but also impersonal and detached. You could assume whatever you liked about a supreme being based on what you see in nature. If, for instance, you live in Australia, you might assume that this force wants you dead given the sheer number of venomous snakes, spiders, and other critters that exist there. Though an entirely different assumption could be drawn from the same context of life Down Under, to quote my Aussie friend, Chris, "This force is tempering us for some form of greatness in the world—conditioning us for supremacy." Given only one lens through which to contemplate existence, you could be forgiven if your perception turns out to be skewed. Such speculation isn't inherently bad, though it may be incomplete.

The Bible, however, gives us more than physical evidence about this *Elohim*, about God. If he did not tell us about himself, we would be left to our suspicions about him, knowing nothing for certain except perhaps a vague sense that he exists. The Westminster Shorter Catechism states, "The Scriptures principally teach what man is to believe concerning God, and what duty God requires of man,"[4] and "The Baptist Faith and Message, 2000" begins with a declaration about the Bible: "The Holy Bible was written by men divinely inspired and is God's revelation of Himself to man. It is a perfect treasure of divine instruction."[5] Each document provides an orthodox understanding of what the Bible is, a pathway to learning more about the God of the universe. Tracking down through thousands of years of history, the Bible's earthly authors narrate the events of God's choice to make himself known.

Why?

God revealed himself because he wants to be known and worshiped.

The God of the universe desires to be seen as the Author of all life, as the primary Cause. There is nothing God cannot and has not provided, and in order for mankind to correctly ascribe to him the glory and credit he deserves, he revealed himself to mankind so that no one or thing would otherwise receive or claim it. Through the Bible, God peels back the curtain to shed light on honey, warm sand between your toes, shifting breezes on sweltering summer evenings, hoar-frost-covered firs, trickling brooks in forest glades, shoulders to rest your head against, and long draughts of cool water. Think about it. Can anyone or anything hold a candle to the creative beauty, complexity, and power that could conceive and make manifest both the visible spectrum of light and the emotions stirred when the very same spectrum of light brings the multifaceted artistry of a sunrise over the ocean to pass? As we read through Scripture, God communicates that he is more than a behind-the-scenes force who brought about the universe and is letting it run its course. The Creator of the universe, beginning with this display of power in Genesis 1, tells his story and it is a story with a simple purpose—to inspire people to worship him.

---

4. "Westminster Shorter Catechism," https://prts.edu/wp-content/uploads/2016/12/Shorter_Catechism.pdf.

5. "The Baptist Faith and Message, 2000," https://bfm.sbc.net/bfm2000.

God's Plan in Creation

God makes himself known through what has been created (Rom 1:19–20) and then tells us about himself through the Scriptures (2 Tim 3:16–17; Heb 1:1) to display that he is worthy of our worship. Just as God crafted the grandeur of the living world, he crafted the human heart, placing in each person a disposition to worship. As the author of Ecclesiastes writes, ". . . he has put eternity into man's heart, yet so that he cannot find out what God has done from the beginning to the end" (3:11). Our finite minds cannot comprehend the infinite and boundless God, but he instilled within us a longing to know and an urge to bow down. In Exodus 20, as God lays out the law by which he wants his people to live, he begins with a proclamation that says much about both his nature and the nature of people.

> I am the Lord your God, who brought you out of the land of Egypt, out of the house of slavery. You shall have no other gods before me. You shall not make for yourself a carved image, or any likeness of anything that is in heaven above, or that is in the earth beneath, or that is in the water under the earth. You shall not bow down to them or serve them, for *I the* Lord *your God am a jealous God*, visiting the iniquity of the fathers on the children to the third and fourth generation of those who hate me, but showing steadfast love to thousands of those who love me and keep my commandments. (Exod 20:2–6, emphasis added)

God's law begins by separating acceptable and unacceptable worship. God gave us a penchant for it and so he set the rules over it.

God's creation is stunning and points to something transcendent behind it, but he doesn't want people to look just anywhere or settle for just any answer. He alone is to be the object of worship and he doesn't share that kind of praise. He tells us he is a jealous God because he is. Now, in our minds, *jealousy* carries a negative connotation. We become jealous of someone because they have something we desire. We connect the term with covetousness and envy, things that we know are unhealthy.

The Blueprint of Grace

God's jealousy, however, is unlike ours. God's jealousy is warranted. The Bible shows us that nothing else in existence is worthy of our worship. People are flawed. Material things fade and decay. As such, God's jealousy over matters of worship centers all of life in the frame of his glory. It was his prerogative to shape the universe in such a way as to get your attention. He could have woven the fabric of reality to hide his presence. He could have remained a distant and far-off God, but he didn't.

He made himself known.

In order to fully comprehend that mystery, you have to embrace it. John Frame writes, "If we are to know God, it is important for us to seek knowledge in God's own way. Many have tried to gain knowledge of God through their unaided reason, or through some kind of subjective intuition. But the God of the Bible has told us not only who he is but also how we should seek knowledge of him."[6] Scripture affixes our understanding of the cosmos to the one who authored it. You have to latch on to what God put forward in his word as truth. Such an act does not ignore or attempt to discredit science. Instead, it measures science against Scripture, recognizing that explaining the system does not equate to understanding the rationale behind it.

My brain can decode the color green because God designed everything in the universe so that when I subconsciously pondered why I knew the color green, I would I consider the elaborate physiological and neurological system that made such a revelation possible and look beyond what is seen to what is unseen to the praise of the one who authored something from nothing.

You exist because he wants you to and he wants you to look for answers. He wants you to understand who he is and who you are in relation to him.

So let's talk about what that's all about.

---

6. Frame, "Divine Revelation," https://www.thegospelcoalition.org/essay/divine-revelation-god-making-known.

2

God's Plan for Mankind

To the choirmaster: according to The Gittith. A Psalm of David.
O Lord, our Lord, how majestic is your name in all the earth! You have set your glory above the heavens. Out of the mouth of babies and infants, you have established strength because of your foes, to still the enemy and the avenger. When I look at your heavens, the work of your fingers, the moon and the stars, which you have set in place, what is man that you are mindful of him, and the son of man that you care for him? Yet you have made him a little lower than the heavenly beings and crowned him with glory and honor. You have given him dominion over the works of your hands; you have put all things under his feet, all sheep and oxen, and also the beasts of the field, the birds of the heavens, and the fish of the sea, whatever passes along the paths of the seas. O Lord, our Lord, how majestic is your name in all the earth!

—Psalm 8

The Blueprint of Grace

I LOVE PSALM 8.

Verses 3–4 particularly captivate me: "When I look at your heavens, the work of your fingers, the moon and the stars, which you have set in place, what is man that you are mindful of him, and the son of man that you care for him?" They help me take stock of what happens to me when I step through my front door and pay attention to what's going on around me. Psalm 8 engenders a kinship of sorts between myself and the author, David. I can feel his joy and his wonder as he takes in the world around him and processes through the one who made it. Not only does David come to terms with his own insignificance in relation with this omnipotent creator, but the psalm demonstrates his awe at even being regarded as worthy of being known by him.

Growing up, I heard a lot about King David from my Sunday school teachers. He was the guy I heard about most often. He was hailed as a great king, a wonderful musician, and a "man after God's own heart." As a guy, such a nickname made me want to sit up and take notice and maybe pattern myself after him. The people teaching me about him certainly presented him as such.

But then I read his story. Start to finish.

I wasn't as enthralled with what I uncovered. The portrait painted by Scripture didn't strike me as one I wanted to model myself after. I was shocked by what I read, particularly concerning his relationship with Bathsheba and how he treated her husband. I reacted like David did to the prophet Nathan's parable about a rich man stealing the precious lamb of a poor man—with indignation. Maybe I wasn't a kindred spirit with the guy who wrote Psalm 8 after all. I turned to him looking for some perfect example of what it looks like to be a human being who was totally sold out for God and found instead a depraved, self-centered dude.

This adulterer wrote most of the Psalms?

This murderer amassed victory after victory in the name of God?

This is what it looks like to be a man after God's own heart?

How was that possible?

No way. That can't be right.

Can it?

But there was something about him that I just couldn't shake. Something deep down inside of me balled up in anger when I read his story. Simultaneously, a small part of me wanted to hide in embarrassment, and not in some sympathetic, "How embarrassing for you" kind of way. He stirred my anger because he knew better but couldn't seem to get it right, but he aroused my shame because I was no different. I felt like his sins were my sins. I could relate much more deeply with them than I cared to acknowledge.

Teenage me knew the right thing to do, just the same as the people you find in the Bible. I knew not to lie, yet I did, particularly about homework. I knew that Jesus said lusting after a woman was as grievous as committing adultery, but my teenage self was drawn to pornography and its insatiable and thoroughly unsatisfying allure. I knew that Proverbs commended industriousness and decried sloth, but I would stay up late goofing off and wake up well after hitting my snooze button for the seventeenth time. Deep down, I rejected what I should do in favor of what was easy, what was fun, what was pleasurable, what cost me the least.

I felt like a fraud because who I thought I was on the inside was not what came out of me on a day-to-day basis. I wondered if I really was saved because if I was, shouldn't I be getting better at following Jesus? Why was I so much like all of the sinners I read about in the pages of Scripture? As much as I wanted to identify with Paul and Peter and James and John, I found myself identifying with the less savory types, the Pharisees and Sadducees and Zealots.

Passages like Philippians 2:14–16 triggered my anxiety. "Do all things without grumbling or disputing, *that you may be blameless and innocent, children of God without blemish* in the midst of a crooked and twisted generation, among whom you shine as lights in the world, holding fast to the word of life, so that in the day of Christ I may be proud that I did not run in vain or labor in vain" (emphasis added). I grew uneasy reading my Bible. If Christians are to be above reproach, why were all of these biblical characters such scumbags? Further still, as I looked around the people who were sitting in church with me, why were they all such scumbags? Beyond that, why was I such a scumbag? Who *was* I?

Was I the guy who wanted to do the right thing or was I the guy who did the wrong thing?

I had an image crisis, one that dates back to the very beginning, when God set out what he wanted for his creation.

God gives mankind an identity . . .

In Genesis 1:1–25, God creates the world and everything in it. He displays his power and his ingenuity and creativity through all of these extremely complex systems and organisms, mammals and fish and birds, and yet it is somehow incomplete. So on day six, he adds one more special piece, different from all the others, a someone rather than a something. "Let us make man in *our image*."(Gen 1:26, emphasis added).

The Master over all matter, the one who formed it with mere words, the Power who tells the sea where to stop encroaching on the land, marked human beings with his image as a testimony to his power and goodness. It is almost impossible put a finger precisely on what it means to be made in the image of God, but that doesn't make it any less true. There is a dignity behind humanity that comes from being crafted in the image of the most creative Force in all of existence. Amazingly, the world gravitates to an understanding of the value and dignity of a person, a characteristic stated plainly in the founding document of the United States: "We hold these truths to be self-evident, that all men are created equal, that they are endowed by their Creator with certain unalienable Rights, that among these are Life, Liberty and the pursuit of Happiness."[1] Three words stand out to me in this explanation of the dignity and value of human life: "All"—everyone; man, woman, child, black, white, rich, poor, whatever; "created"—not evolved, not self-made; and "equal"—no one is either more or less valuable and important than any other.

---

1. "Declaration of Independence," https://www.archives.gov/founding-docs/declaration-transcript.

Yet, over the years, people have committed countless atrocities denying the inherent dignity of a human being. Historically, people have been treated differently, denigrated, and dismissed outright simply because of the color of their skin or their gender or their heritage. We know names like Hitler; groups like the Klu Klux Klan; terms like "ethnic cleansing"; and words like *genocide*, *terrorism*, and *abortion* because we have forgotten the significance of the individual. And immediately, we call it what it is: tragic, abusive, and evil.

But often we fail to get under the surface of why we see it so. Lives cut short or opportunities denied are an affront of some sort because, ultimately, we inherently view people as important. There is something about the way we were created that causes us to want to protect the vulnerable and help the oppressed. Human beings are intrinsically valuable because by their very existence, knowingly and unknowingly, they reflect God into the world around them.

It's a bit like my children. If you've ever looked at my daughters' faces, you will know they carry my wife's genes. In my wife's hometown, people can tell they are my father-in-law's grandchildren just by looking at them. But simultaneously, if you look at their hands and feet, they are unmistakably my children too. They have the same long, slender fingers and both have water skis for feet. Lucy and Daisy are little copies of me and Mandy; they carry our image with them. When they look in the mirror, they see us. When they're out in the world, they represent our presence. Neither would exist without us. That's not arrogance. That's a biological fact. Beyond the scientific evidence of the genetic material that supplies their existence, they demonstrate much more; they reflect back to the world everything that we are as parents. There is much that you can tell about how we treat our children by how they look, but also by how they act. Whatever you discover when you spend some time around our girls tells you as much about us as it does about them.

In the same way that a child reflects his or her parents into the world, humanity reflects information about God. John Piper put it this way: "If you create an image, if you make a sculpture

The Blueprint of Grace

of someone, you do it to display something about that someone . . . Now what would it mean if you created seven billion statues of yourself and put them all over the world? It would mean you would want people to notice you. God created us in his image so that we would display or reflect or communicate who he is, how great he is, and what he is like."[2]

Such is the life of an image-bearer. God coded mankind with an identity based in him and his goodness. So what's the problem?

God gives mankind an identity and a purpose . . .

Mankind's identity is purposeful. Given to be part of God's demonstration to the world that he exists, this *imago Dei*, as it's called, is closely aligned with God's purpose for bestowing it in the first place. Human beings were created in God's image to demonstrate to the cosmos who he is. Larry Crabb writes, "By design, we are called to uniquely express something of him by how we live and relate in our world."[3] But what does it look like to be an image-bearer? Man's acceptable and appropriate representation of God and his interests is defined by God's first command, *"Be fruitful and multiply and fill the earth and subdue it, and have dominion* over the fish of the sea and over the birds of the heavens and over every living thing that moves on the earth." (Gen 1:28, emphasis added). God fashioned mankind for a practical purpose, not on a willy-nilly whim, and gave them his blessing and the responsibility to prosper, to multiply, and to rule over creation. Robin, bee, fish, crab, lion, moose, oak, red bud, tulip, fescue, spider, gnat, camel, sloth, falcon, shag-bark hickory—you name it, mankind was to have authority over it.

---

2. John Piper, "What Does It Mean to Be Made in God's Image?" Ask Pastor John, Desiring God, August 19, 2013, https://www.desiringgod.org/interviews/what-does-it-mean-to-be-made-in-gods-image.

3. Crabb, Hudson, and Andrews, *The Silence of Adam: Becoming Men of Courage in a World of Chaos*, (Grand Rapids, MI: Zondervan Pub. House, 1995), 79.

God's Plan for Mankind

But don't miss this important detail: God didn't give mankind any special equipment or training to carry out his purpose. He merely made him in his image and said, "This is enough. Be blessed as you engage in the work I've given you to do." God knows that at some level human beings are up to the task. No matter how unworthy of his confidence or trust we may occasionally feel, God created us with the necessary ability to do the work. But the heart of the task of the image-bearer lies in the connection with the one whose image he bears.

In any job, you have to follow the company line on how you dress, on how you speak to customers, and the like. If you want to remain employed, then you have to constantly reflect the ethos of the company for which you work. Chick-fil-A is well known for their customer service. They train their "team members" (they're not called "employees") with the understanding that they represent not their individual name on their name tag, but the global brand. The success of the company stems from doing two things extremely well: having fantastic team members and making tremendous chicken. Anyone can make their chicken sandwich; it is literally a fried chicken breast on a buttered bun with a couple of pickle slices. They have a much harder time duplicating the very thing that keeps people coming back for more: the culture of the company. The company's goal is not just to fill customers' stomachs, but give customers a great experience. That vision shows because it is an integral aspect of how each individual franchise operates. The team members reflect what the business is about: good chicken and great service. I readily admit that sometimes the food is not as good as other times, but if you ever have a bad customer service experience at a Chick-fil-A, something has gone wrong, terribly wrong. You can't unhitch the vision of the company from the team members' buy-in. If a team member rejects the company's policies or values, the company will fail and the employee will be fired. However, as team members reflect and carry out the vision and purpose of the company, both employer and employee are applauded and celebrated.

Similarly, God's purpose to be known and worshiped in the world is intimately linked to his vision in bestowing his *imago Dei* to humanity. But God doesn't force man's hand. God intended for humanity to be his stewards over everything he spoke into existence and so he created mankind with the ability to reason and decide and choose. He imbues man with his image and assigns man a task connected to that image. Then he allows man the freedom to decide for himself whether or not to remain aligned with God's vision.

The test of whether or not mankind would stay aligned came early.

God gives mankind an identity and a purpose and a choice.

"You may surely eat of every tree of the garden, but of the tree of the knowledge of good and evil you shall not eat, for in the day that you eat of it you shall surely die" (Gen 2:16–17).

Amidst the multitudes of yes—"every tree of the garden"—God gave exactly *one* no. The text of Genesis informs us that Adam was alone in hearing God's command, so circumstances necessitated an earnest conversation in order to safeguard his beloved "flesh of my flesh," Eve. In my head it went something like this: "Hey babe, we've been blessed with this amazing place to live in. Everything we could ever want is right here. But, there's one little thing we have to avoid. See that tree over there . . ." Adam loved Eve. He cherished this special creation made from his own body. His eyes near popped out of his head with excitement when God presented her to him. Whatever else we think about their relationship, we know Adam told her *something* about God's inclusive-of-many-but-exclusive-of-one rule through what we see in Genesis 3.

> Now the serpent was more crafty than any other beast of the field that the Lord God had made.
>
> He said to the woman, "Did God actually say, 'You shall not eat of any tree in the garden'?"

God's Plan for Mankind

> And the woman said to the serpent, "We may eat of the fruit of the trees in the garden, but God said, 'You shall not eat of the fruit of the tree that is in the midst of the garden, neither shall you touch it, lest you die.'"
> But the serpent said to the woman, "You will not surely die. For God knows that when you eat of it your eyes will be opened, and you will be like God, knowing good and evil."
> So when the woman saw that the tree was good for food, and that it was a delight to the eyes, and that the tree was to be desired to make one wise, she took of its fruit and ate, and she also gave some to her husband who was with her, and he ate. (Gen 3:1–6)

On the surface, it doesn't seem so bad. After all, Adam and Eve were rational beings who could think for themselves. It feels logical that Eve, and subsequently Adam, would want to make good decisions, right? Note how the author of Genesis describes Eve's decision: "So when the woman saw that the tree was good for food, and that it was a delight to the eyes, and that the tree *was to be desired to make one wise*, she took of its fruit and ate" (v. 6, emphasis added). The fruit was good for multiple reasons, but in this moment, everything goes akimbo.

Note their response: "Then the eyes of both were opened, and they knew that they were naked. And they sewed fig leaves together and made themselves loincloths. And they heard the sound of the LORD God walking in the garden in the cool of the day, and the man and his wife hid themselves from the presence of the LORD God among the trees of the garden" (Gen 3:7–8). Instantly, they know something is off. They panic. They hide their nakedness. They cower in fear from the one who gave them life. They have strayed from their purpose. It has as much to do with Adam disobeying God's command to take dominion over creation as God's command not to eat fruit from the tree of the knowledge of good and evil. Endowed with the image of God, Adam possesses the authority and permission and ability to govern, and he abdicates that responsibility. Adam was present. He had means and motive to intervene, yet, for whatever reason, he didn't stop the serpent.

The Blueprint of Grace

Instead, he ceded the dominion granted to him by his Creator through to the very nature he was designed to subdue.

At the heart of this eternity-altering moment is the question, "Who is in charge?" The serpent planted a seed off doubt in Eve's mind with a simple question: "Did God actually say, 'You shall not eat of any tree in the garden?'" It wasn't about nourishment, it was about self-determination. His goal wasn't to twist Eve's words but to subvert God's authority by explaining how the fruit of the tree would make Eve like God, able to govern herself apart from him. C. S. Lewis perhaps explains it best:

> The moment you have a self at all, there is a possibility of putting yourself first—wanting to be the centre—wanting to be God, in fact. That was the sin of Satan: and that was the sin he taught the human race. . .What Satan put into the heads of our remote ancestors was the idea that they 'could be like Gods'—could set up on their own as if they had created themselves—be their own masters—invent some sort of happiness for themselves outside God, apart from God.[4]

Eve attempted to satisfy worldly cravings given to her by her Creator: the pursuit of beauty, a full belly, and the ability to choose well. God designed this complex, multifaceted system of existence so that living under his headship could portray his glory. God created us with bodies in need of nourishment. He gave us inquisitive minds curious for answers. But, make no mistake, fulfilling a God-given desire in a God-prohibited way lies at the core of sin. In opting to satiate that hunger outside of the boundary God put in place, Eve's exercise in autonomy rejected God's vision for her freedom.

Therein lies the challenge.

Every decision provides an opening to violate the desire of the one who created everything. Mutiny lies just beneath the boundless opportunities to exercise our God-given autonomy. C. S. Lewis again comments, "Every time you make a choice you are turning the central part of you, the part of you that chooses, into something a little different from what it was before. And taking

---

4. Lewis, *Mere Christianity*, 49.

your life as a whole, with all your innumerable choices, all your life long you are slowly turning this central thing into a heavenly creature or into a hellish creature."[5] The constant barrage of options numbs diligence, shortening attention spans until absentmindedness takes over. Just as we become nose-blind to the inundating smell of ourselves, we can become decision-blind because of the sheer volume of them we make unconsciously each day.

This reality-blindness stems from a lack of awareness. So does our sinful tendency to be like our ancestors to self-determine. We are forgetful. We forget to remember the truth about who we are, about how God has made us, about why God made us.

It turns out that my identity crisis, my struggle between who I thought I was and who my actions revealed me to be, stemmed from a forgetfulness. All of my bad choices do. I forget that I am made in the image of God. I forget that God blessed me with his likeness to reflect his goodness into the world. I forget to take dominion of my own self, letting my fleshly desires rule over me instead of me ruling over them.

I'm not alone in my struggle. You fight that battle too, and it's not going away. And that's the trouble: we're always one moment from the wrong choice.

Thankfully, God had a plan for that.

---

5. Lewis, *Mere Christianity*, 92.

3

God's Plan through Jesus

And the scribes of the Pharisees, when they saw that he was eating with sinners and tax collectors, said to his disciples, "Why does he eat with tax collectors and sinners?" And when Jesus heard it, he said to them, "Those who are well have no need of a physician, but those who are sick. I came not to call the righteous, but sinners."

—Mark 2:16–17

Grace. God's unmerited favor. It seems simple enough.

Growing up in a charismatic church, I had been taught that to satisfy God I had to be perfect, or at least that is how I heard it. So I tried, again and again, to be perfect. I had come to believe that grace was for when I didn't measure up to God's standard, for when I sinned. After all, I had heard that Jesus came to save sinners—John 3:16 and all that jazz, right? It is true enough, though it doesn't explain the situation fully, because I didn't consider myself a sinner. I considered myself a good person who happened to sin from time to time. Apparently, the umpteen times I had the

God's Plan through Jesus

"Romans Road" of salvation explained to me, particularly the part that says, "For all have sinned and fall short of the glory of God" (Rom 3:23), were not enough.

So, I strove to be righteous under my own steam, but I got frustrated because I couldn't quite get it done. I poured lots of energy into bungled attempts at holiness. I tried hard, but "try hard" isn't the path of success. It's a bit like learning how to throw a slider. You can have an idea how to do it, how to grip the ball and how to release it to produce the right kind of spin, but the more you try and make it break, the more you try and force it to do something, the less likely it is to actually do it. There are physics at play and to be successful you can't manipulate them; you have to trust them. In fact, it's not about trying harder but trusting the science. I could make a concerted, sincere effort and occasionally produce something that resembled holiness, some pale comparison, some whisper of it, but it wasn't the genuine article. I knew what I wanted to do and but I was not able to carry it through. It was a hopeless place to find myself. My life was not sinful due to a lack of desire for holiness, but a lack of ability to achieve it.

The ever-present gap between "want to" and "can do" plagues all of our efforts to be righteous on our own. So what do we do about it?

This is where grace comes in. Our efforts will never be enough. The more we strive for righteousness on our own, the more elusive it becomes.

Benjamin Franklin identified thirteen virtues that he believed to be essential for a good character. He set out to work on them, one at a time. As he found success in one, he would then move to work on the next in his list. What he found, though, was that his efforts at the subsequent virtue would overshadow his attempts at mastering the previous one, and he would forget the prior through intently focusing on the latter. The problem is that as we work toward holiness on our own, we increase the burden to achieve it for ourselves.

The apostle Paul warns the Galatian church about the danger of trying to keep the law for salvation, admonishing them for

The Blueprint of Grace

deserting grace and faith as they turn toward a sense of duty. His message is simply that if you want to try and live by the law, you'd better be perfect and blameless with respect to it. It's an impossible task and Paul stresses that to attempt to rely on a single part of it for justification before God is to subject yourself to the entire law, all of its weight and all of its requirements. If you're relying on your own ability, you cannot misstep, not even once. A single error in judgment, a moment of anger, or a careless word over the course of a lifetime and you become separated from God, your perfection lost.

Think that through. Even when you were a kid and your cerebral cortex wasn't finished developing and you didn't have the impeccable, well-developed emotional control and stability that you quite obviously have now. That one time you cussed out your teacher under your breath for calling you out in front of the class because you didn't do your homework or were passing notes or otherwise disrupting the rest of the class? You're doomed. That time you lied to your parents about why you were late coming home? Same deal. That time as a teenager, or college student, or adult, when you secretly hoped that you'd catch a glimpse of something when your classmate or coworker leaned over? Sin. When you threw subtle shade to your friends about the girl with the ragged hems and dirty hair? Condemned.

Are you getting the picture yet?

You and I face a thoroughly futile task. We have a hard enough time being righteous for a moment or two when we're trying to, so how can we possibly hope that we could pull it off perfectly for a lifetime? The task is Sisyphean, if you will. The will to choose presents us the opportunity to get it right or to make a mess of things. While we can choose well sometimes, the inability to choose well every time is what gets us in trouble. Yet, it is this power of a discerning mind that makes us special. It is what makes us human beings. But whatever benefit we gain from being able to choose becomes a curse because we bungle it.

Thankfully, God has not abandoned us to our ineptitude. Though we are ships with breached hulls, God has a plan to rescue us rather than let us sink to the bottom. He intervenes with grace, a beautiful blessing of favor bestowed on people who neither earn nor deserve it.

God demonstrated grace in the garden...

Right from the beginning, God demonstrates grace. Just three chapters into the story of the Bible, Adam and Eve stretch out and partake of the *one* tree prohibited by the one who made them. There was one rule. The consequence for breaking it was clear, death. Once Adam and Eve recognize their error, in their fear, they try to hide their presence and nakedness through their own efforts by cowering in the bushes and sewing together garments made from fig leaves.

And they're right to do so.

The presence of God is terrifying because his holiness exposes the sins of our hearts. Darkness cannot stand in the overwhelming brightness of God's righteousness. It vanishes, unmade by his pure light. It's why when Isaiah has a vision of the throne room of God, he cries out, "Woe is me! For I am lost; for I am a man of unclean lips, and I dwell in the midst of a people of unclean lips; for my eyes have seen the King, the LORD of hosts!" (Isa 6:5). Sin is undone in the presence of God. The first couple knew they were wrong and knew where their decision had led them—death.

But instead of instant death, God explains the consequences for their actions. It's a little different than what I expected, if I'm honest. Instead of smiting them on the spot, he tells them that life is going to change forever, pronouncing a curse on the serpent, a curse on women, and a curse on men. But even in the hardships that God describes, grace is on display.

First, God shows his favor by not allowing Adam and Eve to walk around shamefully exposed, clothing their nakedness, which is the outward display of their shame. When God creates garments for them, it stands as a reminder that their own efforts to cover their shame are insufficient. John Piper put it this way:

The Blueprint of Grace

> (God) is saying, You are not what you were and you are not what you ought to be. The chasm between what you are and what you ought to be is huge. Covering yourself with clothing is a right response to this—not to conceal it, but to confess it. Henceforth, you shall wear clothing, not to conceal that you are not what you should be, but to confess that you are not what you should be . . . God rejected their own self-clothing. Then he did it himself. He showed mercy with superior clothing.[1]

God covers the sin of Adam and Eve, providing a redemption they could not secure through their own efforts. It is God's first provision for sin and it's a clear demonstration that man cannot cover for his own sin, but it's followed immediately by more grace.

After he covers their shame from their failure to obey, God escorts Adam and Eve out of Eden for their benefit, ensuring they cannot sneak back in to eat from the tree of life. "Then the LORD God said, 'Behold, the man has become like one of us in knowing good and evil. Now, lest he reach out his hand and take also of the tree of life and eat, and live forever'—therefore the LORD God sent him out from the garden of Eden to work the ground from which he was taken" (Gen 3:22–23). By preventing the original sinners from partaking in a fruit that was never previously forbidden from them, God kept them from falling even further away from his presence.

It seems severe, a life spent away from Eden filled with hardship and relational strife. It doesn't look or feel like grace, but is most certainly is grace because the alternative is worse. If Adam and Eve had reached out and eaten from the tree of life, they would never die, banished from God's presence in perpetuity. To live eternally separated from God is literally hell.

God's grace, his favor, extends to those who rejected his authority by choosing to try and govern themselves apart from his input. It's grace because it is unearned; in fact, it goes further.

---

1. Piper, "Rebellion of Nudity," https://www.desiringgod.org/articles/the-rebellion-of-nudity-and-the-meaning-of-clothing.

Adam and Eve earned death, but God instead, in his goodness, provided them a hard life.

After pushing the first couple out of the garden of Eden, God didn't adjust his scorecard or start grading on the curve; he didn't look out on the world, realize that imperfect people couldn't behave perfectly, and say, "Oh well, this will have to do." The through line is that God calls people, time and time again, to be obedient; his standard hasn't changed.

The cycle repeats over and over. God makes provision and mankind perverts it, taking God's good gifts and twisting them to their own ends. From Genesis 4 to Genesis 50, the story keeps moving forward and though the names change, the behaviors don't. People still get it right from time to time and still mess up far more often than they would like. This is what life is like after the fall. People are imperfect and their imperfection shows up in major ways. Through it all, as people wander away from obedience to satisfy off-limits hankerings, God provides opportunity to return to him. Even though the people don't deserve grace, God is a good God. Man makes some good decisions and some really bad ones too, but the through line remains: God's standard is still perfect obedience.

God demonstrated grace in the garden, pointed to grace through the Law of Moses . . .

At the end of Genesis, God's chosen people find themselves living in Egypt as God has richly blessed them, working through a faithful man who trusted that God was good, Joseph, the son of Jacob, the son of Isaac, the son of Abraham. Then we basically lose track of the story for about three hundred or so years, but it picks up again with this one family's descendants, called the Israelites, imprisoned and enslaved in Egypt. In the midst of their oppression, this one family has grown to massive numbers and they cry out for deliverance to the God of their fathers, Abraham, Isaac, and Jacob. God hears their lamentation, their sobbing, their wailing over their mistreatment and, in his goodness, responds by raising up Moses to lead his people out of captivity in miraculous fashion.

Through Moses, God brings his people out of slavery and begins leading them toward the land that he promised to Abraham. It's a difficult and wearying journey, but they're free. The Israelites grumble about what they don't have while they're on their trek, but rather than wipe them out in frustration about their ingratitude for rescuing them from captivity, God provides, again and again. Eventually, God calls the entire assembly of Israel to draw near to him at Mount Sinai and he makes a deal with them. "You yourselves have seen what I did to the Egyptians, and how I bore you on eagles' wings and brought you to myself. Now therefore, if you will indeed obey my voice and keep my covenant, you shall be my treasured possession among all peoples, for all the earth is mine; and you shall be to me a kingdom of priests and a holy nation" (Exod 19:4–6).

At the heart of his promise to be their God and they his people lies obeying God's voice and keeping his covenant.

Through Moses, God establishes two systems: one, a system of outward codes of conduct concerning diet, dress, and the like; and second, a complex system of offerings and sacrifices for when they fail to uphold the aforementioned codes of conduct. Pervasive and thorough, these standards provided the Israelites a moment-by-moment opportunity to carry the weight of being counted as God's people. God gives the Israelites the same choice that he gave to Adam and Eve—obedience or disobedience. Through the law, God set the rules for his people. By requiring a lot, he drives home the obedience he desires and indeed is due, but also makes provision for disobedience through the sacrificial system. Reading through Exodus, Leviticus, and Numbers, it feels like the Israelites spent as much time making peace, burnt, grain, sin, and guilt offerings as they did plowing, reaping, or sowing their fields. In short, God provided a sacrificial system to remind the people that they were in need of restoration and reconciliation.

The two systems, taken in their entirety as the "Law," give shape to the people's response to the reality that God's commitment to them is an equally binding commitment to him. God doesn't lord his authority over the Israelites, demanding their respect and admiration because of his provision, but the Israelites' dedication to God would always be on display through their adherence to things that set them apart from the cultures around them.

What follows is a thousand or so years of God's people flip-flopping back and forth from closely following him and utterly abandoning him. A cyclical pattern develops and repeats again and again: life is good, and people decide they want something beyond God's bounds for them; forgetting God's standard of obedience, they pursue it and reap the consequences of their choices. Their disobedience is worthy of death. God would be justified in wiping his people out and starting over yet again, but he refuses to leave people to their fate. The sacrificial system, the shedding of blood, covers over the sins of the people.

When he pushed Adam and Eve out of Eden, he covered the outward evidence of their sin and shame with garments of animal skin. Similarly, when he gave the Israelites the Law with the code of conduct, God accentuated that the standard will always be obedience to his commands, and through the sacrificial system he continued to provide a method of redemption from disobedience. And through the centuries, despite the self-destructive tendencies of his people, God never left nor forsook them. What he provided the first couple and his people are mere shadows of what came next.

God demonstrated grace in the garden, pointed to grace through the Law of Moses, and manifested grace in Jesus.

Throughout the self-destructive tendencies of his people, God never left them nor forsook them. He always sent messengers in the form of prophets to help people interpret the times, to help them see the error of their ways, so they would turn back to him. Would God be just in wiping people out and starting over? He sure would, but he refused to leave people to their fate.

The Blueprint of Grace

Some 1,500 years after Moses leads the Israelites out of Egypt and into the wilderness toward the promised land, a millennia and a half after God gave his people a code of conduct that pointed to their constant need of his intervention, things change. The Old Testament ends with a remnant of the Israelites settled in a portion of the promised land, a small but significant portion. Then, for four and a half centuries, there is radio silence from God. But then something unusual happens. God speaks again; this time not by some old prophet.

The apostle John tells us that the Word of God, whom we come to find out is Jesus, the Son of Man, the Messiah prophesied in Old Testament, the one who would bruise the head of the serpent, the one by whom and through whom all things were made, stepped out of the supernatural realm and became a human being. "In the beginning was the Word, and the Word was with God, and the Word was God. He was in the beginning with God. All things were made through him, and without him was not any thing made that was made . . . And the Word became flesh and dwelt among us, and we have seen his glory, glory as of the only Son from the Father, full of grace and truth" (John 1:1–2, 14). The author of Hebrews frames it thusly: "Long ago, at many times and in many ways, God spoke to our fathers by the prophets, but in these last days he has spoken to us by his Son, whom he appointed the heir of all things, through whom also he created the world. He is the radiance of the glory of God and the exact imprint of his nature, and he upholds the universe by the word of his power" (Heb 1:1–3). In his letter to the church at Philippi, the apostle Paul adds that Jesus, "who, though he was in the form of God, did not think equality with God a thing to be grasped, but emptied himself, by taking the form of a servant, being born in the likeness of men" (Phil 2:6–7). This fully-God-fully-man hybrid of an individual is the embodiment of God.

Through Jesus, he graciously provides yet again. The second member of the Trinity, the Son, leaves heaven to do the will of the Father, becoming a second Adam. The standard of obedience from the garden of Eden never changed. The first Adam was given the

God's Plan through Jesus

opportunity to be obedient to God, but instead chose to determine his own path to the detriment of all of history. The image of God, perfect at the moment of creation, then marred by Adam's disobedience, is now passed down through his son to all generations. But God's plan to reverse that was to recreate a new humanity through the obedience of Jesus, a second and better Adam. And Jesus accomplishes what Adam did not, what the first man could not—perfect obedience. The solution for man's problem with sin begins with the life of Jesus. And then, after living the life Adam was supposed to live, living the life that all of us are supposed to live, Jesus sealed the victory over sin by choosing to die so that his Father's wrath against sin would be satisfied. Jesus, who never sinned, took the penalty for sin—all of the sins that have ever been committed in the past, are being committed presently, and will be committed in the future. And it wasn't just any kind of death. Jesus died a sinner's death, shamed and crucified publicly on a Roman cross. The shame God covered up for millennia, through garments that proclaimed that mankind wasn't what we should be and through the sacrificial system that made provisions for our shortcomings, was displayed in a profound way.

Stripped, beaten, mocked, scorned, abandoned, and left hanging by his wrists to die, Jesus bore the shame of all mankind to the cross, allowing God's justice to fall upon himself. "For our sake he [God] made him [Jesus] to be sin who knew no sin, so that in him [Jesus] we might become the righteousness of God" (2 Cor 5:21). Upon that instrument of Roman torture, Jesus cried out, "'It is finished,' and he bowed his head and gave up his spirit" (John 19:30). He willingly subjected himself to the standard of God's plan, obedient to God's will even in, and to, his death.

But his death is not the end of the story. If Jesus remained dead, then there is no hope, no victory. Jesus's death for our sins isn't good news without the resurrection.

On the third day, Jesus rises from the grave, overcoming death itself. By emerging from the tomb, Jesus shows that the righteous will not die. While that feels problematic for a people who cannot be righteous, God gifts the righteousness of Jesus to those who

The Blueprint of Grace

admit their need for it. Mankind does not and cannot earn God's favor. We are broken. We don't need to change our behavior; we need to be remade. Yet in his goodness God furnished the means for an unworthy people to be reborn, Jesus, for no other reason than that he was pleased to do so.

Everything changes because of the cross and the empty tomb. There is no need for death because Jesus paid mankind's debt to sin. Through Jesus, the burden of death that lay on all humanity is lifted, because now, rather than living a life in the image of Adam, God credits Jesus' righteousness to those who put their faith in him, thus creating a new humanity, made in the image of Christ rather than the image of Adam.

God sent Jesus to seek and save the lost, to break the bonds of slavery to sin, and to reform the marred and fallen image of man. And he does. It is the free gift of God to those who believe, one available to those who admit their need for it. Because of the cross, God accepts those who would consider Jesus's death their own, those who would put their old self to death, those who would attempt to walk in the newness of life that is found in Christ. He makes a new humanity from every tribe and tongue, fused together through the death, burial, and resurrection of Jesus, reversing the curse of sin and pointing his creation toward a future no longer separated from the Creator.

4

God's Plan through the Holy Spirit

And it is God who establishes us with you in Christ, and has anointed us, and who has also put his seal on us and given us his Spirit in our hearts as a guarantee.

—2 Corinthians 1:21–22

I feel like the beginning of the TV show *Dragnet*: "Ladies and Gentlemen, the story you are about to hear is true. Only the names have been changed to protect the innocent." My personal history of understanding the person and work of the Holy Spirit is tinged with pain and anxiety because of my experiences growing up in various charismatic Pentecostal Christian settings.

Please don't miss this: I don't think the people from my early church years were intentionally teaching things contrary to Scripture, but I do think their beliefs about how God's Spirit operates led to some wonky teaching. I know that my experience may not be normative of a charismatic church, but from conversations with others, my experience is unfortunately not uncommon.

The Blueprint of Grace

For instance, when I was about eight years old, a Sunday school teacher took me into a dark room after I said I wanted to accept Jesus as my Savior. She then proceeded to tell me to pray to ask Jesus into my heart and then to speak in tongues. I had a vague understanding of what that meant. I had heard people in the church service babbling and almost spastically making noises, sounding like a cross between clearing their throats of phlegm, random syllables, and heavy breathing. So, in an effort to prove that I wanted to be saved by Jesus, because I *really* wanted to be saved by Jesus, and to please my Sunday school teacher, I faked it by attempting to replicate the noises I had heard for years. Somehow this woman had convinced me that I had to be able to speak in tongues and I convinced her that I was able to do so. I thought that by consciously generating this incomprehensible speech, I was doing what I needed to do to be accepted into God's family.

Deep down, I wanted to be good enough to be accepted by Jesus and the church, so I put on a facade. I knew I fell short of what God wanted from someone who called himself a believer, but I desperately wanted to be in that number of the saints that go marching in, if you will.

For the next several years, I tried to speak the language and tried to understand what it was about. After all, in the Bible speaking in tongues seems normative, a regular occurrence. Reading through the book of Acts, it is on display as evidence of the change wrought in people's hearts, Jews and Gentiles alike. The Holy Spirit fell on them and they spoke with "heavenly words," outwardly exhibiting what was happening in their souls. And those aren't the only pictures of what the Holy Spirit was doing in Acts. At least, that's how it was presented to me. I was given a snapshot of a single tree and told that all of the trees in the world looked like exactly like this one. It wasn't a poorly drawn representation. In fact, it's a beautiful tree, miraculous even. But it also isn't representative of the fascinating variance of trees in creation.

Decades removed from the closet incident, the Holy Spirit remains a bit of a mystery to me, and to a lot of people. I don't claim to be an expert about him, but I do think the text of the Bible demonstrates that the Holy Spirit works to restore things to their natural order. In fact, throughout Scripture, you can find the Spirit interrupting the "natural" order of things through miracles and prophecy and the like in order to draw people back into a right relationship with God. In the last chapter we saw that we needed grace to fix our relationship with God; grace ultimately manifested through the death, burial, and resurrection of Jesus. If God's role was to initiate salvation for his people and Jesus' role was to accomplish salvation for his people, then the Holy Spirit's role is to apply salvation to his people.

The Holy Spirit awakens our hearts...

Life hasn't always been as it is now.

As God ordered the universe in Genesis 1, shaping chaos into cosmos, he characterized the work as "good." At the end of the sixth day, as he prepared to rest from his creative work, he said it wasn't just good, but "very good" (Gen 1:31). God's design was exactly what he intended. Without flaw, the creation crafted from nothingness existed in perfect harmony and balance. And in that moment, everything was perfect. Life was good, so to speak.

And then the first man and woman brought sin into the world through disobedience. The good of creation didn't last. The fall taints creation itself: "... cursed is the ground because of you; in pain you shall eat of it all the days of your life; thorns and thistles it shall bring forth for you; and you shall eat the plants of the field" (Gen 3:17–18). What was perfect deteriorated, regressing toward its previously disordered state.

From that day, rebellion took root and people, separated from their Creator by their sin, sought to be masters of their own domain. It has led us, through the ages, to explain all of life ignoring and even scorning the divine influence and design of God. The attempts to interpret life reflect the impulse to seek answers. Various mythologies crop up in the world filled by stories of greater powers and gods told by cultures seeking to make sense of the known world. Over the years these tales have given way to theories and

The Blueprint of Grace

laws as science and technology provide flashes of understanding. People are satisfied that the answers can be had if you will only accept the science or grasp the principles. But behind every attempt to understand existence lies the truth that God is constantly working to draw people to himself.

From the very beginning, God built bridges for his creation to find their way back to him. In the Old Testament, we read stories of his provision: an ark for Noah and his family, a heritage for childless Abram and Sarai, a covenant to outline what it means to be in relationship with him. Even as his people stray from that relationship, God sends messenger after messenger, empowered by his Spirit, to correct them and bring them back. Elijah and Elisha perform powerful miracles and proclaim oracles against wicked kings. Jeremiah and Hosea deliver messages of warning to corrupt leaders. Amos delivers the final decrees condemning the actions of those who have perverted justice and neglected the purpose God has given for authority in the Northern Kingdom of Israel. Through all of it, God is creating opportunities for his people to turn back to him.

Then, in the New Testament, we see John the Baptizer with a similar message: "Repent, for the kingdom of heaven is at hand" (Matt 3:2). Jesus himself says that he did not come to judge the world but to save it (John 3:17). The message of Peter after his first sermon on the day of Pentecost concludes with the exhortation, "Repent and be baptized every one of you in the name of Jesus Christ for the forgiveness of your sins, and you will receive the gift of the Holy Spirit. For the promise is for you and for your children and for all who are far off, everyone whom the Lord our God calls to himself" (Acts 2:38–39). The common thread in all of these men is the message and power of the Holy Spirit coming through them. The apostle Peter would later write, "For no prophecy was ever produced by the will of man, but men spoke from God as they were carried along by the Holy Spirit" (2 Pet 1:21). These men of antiquity were not speaking of their own accord, but by the power and will of God himself. Their words were inspired and emboldened by the very Spirit of God. The message "Repent!"

demonstrates just how much God desires to be with his people, how much he desires to show mercy rather than wrath. God could have acted in a similar fashion to when he sent the flood in days of Noah, and he would have been justified to do so, but he doesn't want to destroy. He wants to bless. The greatest blessing is a relationship with him.

Because this relationship is paramount, God does whatever he can to catch people's eye. Consider that thousands flocked to Jesus' teaching and healing. Why? Because he, through the work of the Holy Spirit, brought little pieces of the perfection of heaven to the woefully broken earth. Through Jesus' ministry, the Holy Spirit broke in and gave glimpses that not all is OK in the world by flashing the power to revert things to what is "natural." As Dane Ortlund astutely comments

> We tend to think of the miracles of the Gospels as interruptions in the natural order. Yet German theologian Jurgen Moltmann points out that miracles are not an interruption of the natural order but the restoration of the natural order. We are so used to a fallen world that sickness, disease, pain, and death seem natural. In fact, *they* are the interruption. When Jesus expels demons and heals the sick, he is driving out of creation the powers of destruction, and is healing and restoring created beings who are hurt or sick. The lordship of God to which the healings witness, restores creation to health. Jesus' healings are not supernatural miracles in a natural world. They are the only truly "natural" thing in a world that is unnatural, demonized, and wounded.[1]

God's Spirit stirs up the waters, so to speak. He agitates our hearts by breaking into the fallen world with messages of hope for a world that once existed and in the end will come to be again. His work flits through the world, touching lives in ways we can barely comprehend, but he does so not just to bring a little bit of heaven for our comfort in the here and now; he does it to remind us that things are not as they are supposed to be and that there is a Creator

---

1. Ortlund, *Gentle and Lowly*, 31.

out there, one more powerful than our imagination, one capable of doing far more abundantly than all we could ask or think to ask.

And not only does this God above all the little gods we fashion for ourselves exist; he draws our attention to himself through the work of his Spirit so that we can see the reality of our need of him and his intervention.

The Holy Spirit awakens our hearts, convicts our hearts...

In his last conversation with his disciples, Jesus tells them that he is sending a Helper into the world, a Helper that will convict the world. "And when he comes, he will convict the world concerning sin and righteousness and judgment..." (John 16:8). Throughout history, God's Spirit has been working in many ways and places, through young and old, through his people and the enemies of his people, to bring them back to God the Father. Then God sends his own Son, Jesus, to fulfill his promises to redeem his people, the descendants of Abraham, from their sins. And Jesus performs miracle after miracle, giving sight to the blind, opening the mouths of the mute, cleansing the unclean, even feeding thousands with what we would equate to a couple of Lunchables. But perhaps one of the most profound miracles of Jesus, the one that points us to his true mission on earth, comes pretty early in his ministry.

He is traveling, as Jesus is wont to do, preaching, teaching, healing, caring for those whom no one else cares. One day he is teaching in Capernaum and a crowd gathers to hear him. The crowd is so thick that the house in which he is staying is full and surrounded by a throng of people desperate to see and hear this man from Nazareth. Some have heard of his miraculous power and bring a friend of theirs, a paralytic, to this impromptu gathering, confident that if they can only get him into his presence, he will be healed. Alas, the crush of those trying to draw near to Jesus is too great. So they do what any sane person would do—they climb up onto the roof with their friend! And once they're up there, they remove some of the thatch and lower their friend through the ceiling into the presence of this man who teaches with authority and heals all those who are brought to him. Maybe you know the story and maybe you don't, but what happens next is sudden and mind-blowing. Jesus looks at the man, then looks at his friends who have undertaken such a desperate task, and ". . . when Jesus saw their faith, he said to the paralytic, 'Son, your sins are forgiven'" (Mark 2:5). These people didn't bring their friend to Jesus because of his sins; they came because of his physical infirmities, because they had heard people rejoicing in the miracles Jesus had performed through the region. But Jesus' mission isn't to heal people from their physical maladies in their earthly bodies, but to restore the condition of their spiritually broken souls, which hunger and thirst for righteousness before God. These breakthrough moments of power and restoration of the truly natural, God-designed order are meant to draw people to hear the real message. "Repent, for the kingdom of heaven is at hand."

One of the great verses about Jesus' ministry on earth is found in the Gospel of Mark: "Let us go on to the next towns, that I may preach there also, for that is why I came out" (Mark 1:38). And in Luke 5, Jesus plainly proclaims his message: "Those who are well have no need of a physician, but those who are sick. I have not come to call the righteous but sinners to repentance" (Luke 5:31–32). So who comes to Jesus? Those in need of him, that's who. But how can they come unless they know they need him?

My former senior pastor likes to say that the first thing you have to do to get saved is get lost. How can you possibly turn to God for salvation if you have no idea that, one, you need to be saved and, two, you can be saved? The answer comes from rightly understanding the gravity of the situation, the depth of the problem, and the hopelessness of man's fallen estate. The first step is always admitting there is a problem.

I love how Jesus calls Simon Peter to be his disciple. Simon is a fisherman—has been his entire life. One day he is out futilely casting his nets upon the water. He draws the nets in, and he's got zip, zilch, nada, over and over. And just when he's about to give up, bringing his boat to the shore, this man who has been teaching and healing and performing miracles gets into his boat and tells him to head back out a bit so as to provide a place from which he can teach a gathering crowd. After he gets done teaching, this man says to Simon, "Cast your nets on the port side of the boat rather than the starboard," as if the fish don't swim in all the water, like they knew it was safe on one side of this little fishing skiff on the surface but not the other. It's wild to think about. But Simon, at the request of this teacher and healer, does just that. And he doesn't just catch one or two fish. The haul is so great that it threaten to capsize not just his boat but the boat of his partners as well. When Simon experiences this miracle, he immediately recognizes what is going on and he cries out, "Depart from me, for I am a sinful man, O Lord" (Luke 5:8). Are the fish a blessing? Absolutely! But what lay beneath the miracle is the very power of God, which cuts Simon to the heart. He knows instantly that he is in the presence of God and that he is unworthy. Like Isaiah cries out, "Woe is me! For I am lost; for I am a man of unclean lips, and I dwell in the midst of a people of unclean lips; for my eyes have seen the King, the Lord of hosts!"(Isa 6:5), when he is brought into the throne room of God, Simon Peter sees his greater need is not physical in nature, but spiritual.

This is what the Holy Spirit does in convicting people concerning "sin and righteousness and judgment" (John 16:8). He makes us aware that all is not right, not just in our lives, but in our hearts. He leads us from a place of confidence or striving or hopelessness or desperation and to somewhere we can be overwhelmed by God's grace. We experience grace as the Holy Spirit slices away all of our pretense and all of our posturing, peeling back our defenses to open us up to the reality that we are people who are sick and in need of a doctor. He shows us our need.

When we recognize that we have a problem that we cannot fix, a hole we cannot fill, a relationship we cannot repair, a standard we cannot meet, we are forced to look outside of ourselves. The Holy Spirit captures our attention and directs our gaze outside of our own efforts to justify ourselves. And there we find Jesus, who knows our need and has met it on our behalf. He lived the perfect sinless life you and I and everyone else were supposed to be living from the beginning of time. He alone met God's standard of obedience and he met it perfectly. He did what we could not. Jesus paved the way and then the Holy Spirit enables us to walk that path.

The Holy Spirit awakens our hearts, convicts our hearts, and justifies our hearts.

In the Gospel of John, Jesus has a pretty famous conversation with Nicodemus, a religious teacher and Pharisee:

> Jesus: Truly, truly, I say to you, unless one is born again he cannot see the kingdom of God.
>
> Nicodemus: How can a man be born when he is old? Can he enter a second time into his mother's womb and be born?
>
> Jesus: Truly, truly, I say to you, unless one is born of water and the Spirit, he cannot enter the kingdom of God. That which is born of the flesh is flesh, and that which is born of the Spirit is spirit. Do not marvel that I said to you, "You must be born again." The wind blows where it wishes, and you hear its sound, but you do not know where it comes from or where it goes. So it is with everyone who is born of the Spirit. (John 3:3–8)

It's the predecessor to Jesus' declaration about how much God loves the world. But note, Jesus says that a rebirth must happen. Without God's intervention, everyone is dead, not literally, but spiritually. Of course, without God's intervention, everyone will surely die. It is the great equalizer of mankind. No matter one's wealth or influence or status in life—rich, poor, black, white, male, female, young, old—*everyone* is in the same boat: we are all going to die. The leading cause of death is being born. I have never known anyone ever born who has not or will not die. Have you?

The end of life is death. But in John, Jesus says that in order to enter the kingdom of God, one must be reborn, specifically reborn of the Spirit. It's a strange concept for Nicodemus, but just because we can't understand it doesn't make it less true. In fact, though we

The Blueprint of Grace

can't ever seem to quite get our heads wrapped around the concept of regeneration, and irrespective of whichever order it happens in, what we know for sure is that it is a miracle of God *that* it happens. What was once dead is made alive. But here's one thing you can know for certain: God is the one who makes it all happen. To the Ephesians, the apostle Paul writes, "But God, being rich in mercy, because of the great love with which he loved us, even when we were dead in our trespasses, made us alive together with Christ" (Eph 2:4–5). Made possible by Jesus' death, burial, and resurrection, our new life is in Christ for it is through Christ's perfection that we find our righteousness. David Garner comments, "Due to Christ's sinless, covenantally faithful life, the Father vindicates him, declares him righteous (1 Tim. 3:16). By the agency of the Spirit, believers enjoy Christ's vindication/justification as our own: "you were justified in the name of our Lord Jesus Christ and by the Spirit of our God" (1 Cor. 6:11). *Justification is secured by Jesus; it is applied to us by his Spirit.*"[2] Whatever transactional economics you want to employ, the Spirit takes the righteousness of Christ and justifies those who put their faith in him. It is what makes the gospel the gospel.

Our fight against our sinful nature ended at the cross. Christ finished it there by laying down his perfection and taking up our sins—past, present, and future—as his own. He bled and died to buy our pardon so that when we accept our own futility and his accomplishment on our behalf, the Holy Spirit replaces our sinfulness with his righteousness.

And this is merely the first sliver of what the Spirit of God does in the life of those who trust in Jesus. There is so much more to come, and we will spend the rest of the book dealing with some of it. Some we will not see until the very end of time itself; therefore I will not speculate too much about that. However, between now and then, the Spirit moves and works, continuing to draw those who are far from God, like moths to a flame.

But once we have committed ourselves to God, then what?

To that we now turn our attention.

---

2. Garner, "Holy Spirit: Agent of Salvation," https://www.thegospelcoalition.org/essay/the-holy-spirit-agent-of-salvation/.

Interlude

So now what?

If you've stuck with me this far, you're just now getting to the good stuff.

I mean, we've hit the point where we've covered a lot of the theological framework for who God made us to be, why we're not who God made us to be, and what God has done about the fact that we're not who he made us to be.

These truths bring to mind this question: "If who I used to be isn't who I am now, and who I am now is only the first step in the journey toward who I'm meant to be, how do I become who God meant me to be?"

Well, as I said in the previous chapter, we're all dead in our transgressions apart from God's intervention. Well, those are Paul's words actually.

> And you were dead in the trespasses and sins in which you once walked, following the course of this world, following the prince of the power of the air, the spirit that is now at work in the sons of disobedience—among whom we all once lived in the passions of our flesh, carrying out the desires of the body and the mind, and were by nature children of wrath, like the rest of mankind. (Eph 2:1–3)

But rather than leaving us in that awful state, Paul tells us what God did for us.

The Blueprint of Grace

> But God, being rich in mercy, because of the great love with which he loved us, even when we were dead in our trespasses, made us alive together with Christ—by grace you have been saved—and raised us up with him and seated us with him in the heavenly places in Christ Jesus, so that in the coming ages he might show the immeasurable riches of his grace in kindness toward us in Christ Jesus. For by grace you have been saved through faith. And this is not your own doing; it is the gift of God, not a result of works, so that no one may boast. (Eph 2:4-9)

But as if that isn't enough, God still isn't done with us. Not only does he regenerate our hearts and make us new creations in Christ (2 Cor 5:17); the original mission of mankind, to act accordingly, still holds. "For we are his workmanship, created in Christ Jesus for good works, which God prepared beforehand, that we should walk in them" (Eph 2:10). God still has a plan for us: to do the good works he has called us to do.

So, how do we go about doing that?

I mean, we can't function as we have if we want to be pleasing to God. We have to have a complete shift of who we are in order to change what we do. And the good news is that who we are in Christ is not who we were before Christ. There are a lot of things people can argue about the order of salvation and faith and justification and such topics, but one thing is certain: if you're in Christ, the old you is gone and the new you is here. To the Galatians Paul writes, "I have been crucified with Christ. It is no longer I who live, but Christ who lives in me. And the life I now live in the flesh I live by faith in the Son of God, who loved me and gave himself for me" (Gal 2:20). It's actually something he writes about over and over again in his letters. There's a change that takes place and the life you used to live is not the life you should live going forward.

So let's start talking about what happens now. What happens to a believer after God brings them to repentance from their sins?

5

The Blueprint

Therefore be imitators of God, as beloved children.

—Ephesians 5:1

About one month into the second semester of eighth grade, my industrial arts teacher set a twenty-seven-inch-tall, fifteen-inch-wide, and nine-inch-deep side table on his desk and said, "You're going to build one of these." It wasn't a mid-century modern project, or a fancy mission-style table, or something Victorian. Nope. It was a rectangular cupboard-type table made from white pine 1x10s with a shelf at the bottom and six-inch cubby between the tabletop and a four-inch-deep drawer. Given a pattern and some basic instructions, we cut, sanded, glued, squared, screwed, stained, and sealed the boards, fashioning a usable table. We even learned some tricks for leveling its feet so it wouldn't fall over or teeter around like kids on a playground seesaw. It isn't artistic or beautiful, except in its simplicity and utility. It sits in my living

The Blueprint of Grace

room some thirty-three years later, the drawer in one piece, still sliding in and out smoothly.

The project wasn't hard. If I had the proper tools today, I'd venture it would take me less than a day to replicate and assemble the form and maybe another day or two to stain or lacquer it. It took us the better part of two months, working during a forty-five-minute class period, for two periods a week. Why? Because we didn't know how to use the tools well. We had to be taught, step by step, how to use the bandsaw, the router, the jigsaw, and the belt sander.

At the end of our eight-week project, nearly everyone had finished and those who hadn't had missed days of school. Almost every one of the final products looked similar, though not exactly the same. The colors varied slightly based on the stain and lacquer selected. The edges rolled differently as we all had different tastes in finish and used differing pressures to sand smooth the hewn pieces. In general, however, you could see that we had all begun with the same pattern, despite the variance in results.

If you were to tell a bunch of junior high students to build a bedside table, you might end up with a teenager with one fewer fingertip or a thumbnail mashed by a hammer. You would most definitely end up with a kid going to the nurse because he got sawdust in his eye. But the thing you're most likely to see is brilliant displays of ineptitude. Creative ineptitude, but ineptitude nonetheless.

What made the difference for our class then?

At the outset, the instructor provided for us an example of what we were going to be piecing together. We had a pattern to follow, yes, but rather than letting us sweat over building a bedside table, the teacher showed us a finished product. We had a tangible prototype we could touch and examine closely. We could compare our work to his so we could create our best facsimile.

In the same way, God holds up for us an example of what he wants his followers to become—Christlike. The Bible presents us with an exemplar, the exemplar of righteous living in the personhood of Jesus Christ, and then directs its readers to become more like him. He is the model, the pattern, after which we need to shape our lives. In his first letter to Corinth, Paul writes, "Be imitators of me, as I am of Christ" (1 Cor 11:1). That's not Paul saying he's the paragon—far from it. He is saying, "Look at my life and imitate it because I am imitating Christ as best as I can." As we examine our own failures and imperfections in comparison to the perfectly righteous Christ and then set our minds on leaving behind the former to conform to the latter, we set our course for the next phase of our lives. None of us will do it perfectly, but as the Holy Spirit convicts us of our sins and we repent of them, a new pattern of behavior should emerge; one that looks less and less like who we used to be and more and more like Jesus.

Sanctification begins as we give up who we have been in order to become who God wants us to be.

In Matthew 16, Jesus tells his closest friends that if anyone wants to be his disciple, the first step is self-denial, followed by identifying with his death. "If anyone would come after me, let him deny himself and take up his cross and follow me. For whoever would save his life will lose it, but whoever loses his life for my sake will find it" (Matt 16:24–25). Earlier in Matthew, Jesus says that the way to life is entered through a narrow gate and is a hard journey. Given these words here in Matthew 16, I can see why.

Abandon your self.

Walk away from the life you used to know.

We'll explore this picture more in the coming chapters, but we have to start with the end in mind. In his letter to the church in Rome, Paul writes that God is always shaping those he has saved into a better representation of the one who has saved them. God works to conform his adopted children into the image of his Son, Jesus.

So what does that mean for you and I as Christians? It means that our job is to focus on Jesus. But before you get too far down the track, I want to give you a word of caution about this path: it is hard and it is going to cost you your life. I don't mean that you're going to die because of your faith. You're going to die one way or another, barring a miracle. No, what I mean is that the path Jesus lays out for you in Matthew 16:24–25 is the path he himself walked. Think that through for a moment.

During his earthly life, Jesus constantly talks about how he can only do what he sees the Father doing and how he has a mission which is not his own. Everything Jesus does comes as a direct result of him doing what God wants from him. I know the mental gymnastics it takes to consider how obedience fits into Jesus' life. The author of Hebrews writes that we have a great high priest in heaven who is able to sympathize with us in every way because he was tempted in every way, yet he never sinned. If Jesus is fully man, then of course he was capable of sin; and in the same breath, Jesus was fully God, so could he *really* sin? I'll leave that discussion to theologians much smarter and wiser than me, though for my part I believe he could indeed have chosen, in his humanity, disobedience. But it is crucial to show how that plays out in real time.

As Jesus enters Jerusalem in the last week of his life, looking ahead at what would come his way, he expresses emotion after emotion. He is heralded as he enters Jerusalem. In the next scene Matthew narrates for us, Jesus overturns the tables of those exploiting the financial poverty of his people in the temple. We see righteous anger, gentle correction, pointed teaching, truth-fueled rebuke, and merciful lament. The images and stories flash around the city, each soaked with anticipation of what this prophet from Nazareth might say or do next.

Finally he settles in to observe the Passover with those closest to him, the Twelve. It is a meal mixed with sorrow and love. But after the meal, after Judas Iscariot has departed from the group to betray his rabbi, Jesus takes his dear friends with him to a place outside the city, to the Mount of Olives, to a garden called Gethsemane.

What is it Jesus says? "If anyone would come after me, let him deny himself and take up his cross and follow me" (Matt 16:24). Jesus asks his disciples to pray with him and then he wanders off deeper into the garden to pray by himself. What does he pray? "My Father, if it be possible, let this cup pass from me; nevertheless,

The Blueprint

not as I will, but as you will" (Matt 26:39) Jesus doesn't want to die. He knows what lays ahead. He grasps the physical torment of what will unfold in the next twenty-four hours. He understands the emotional agony he will experience as his friends desert him. In his humanity, Jesus wants nothing to do with any of it.

But he surrenders himself.

He denies himself.

Do not miss this: Jesus of Nazareth chooses to set aside his own physical and emotional well being in order to fulfill the will of the Father—". . . not as I will, but as you will." How hard is it? He has to pray it three times! In verse 42 it says he prays, "My Father, if this cannot pass unless I drink it, your will be done." And then in verse 44 he prays once more, the same words, and I am blown away when I read them. Jesus denies himself. He denies his flesh, which screams, "I want to live! I don't want to suffer!" Every atom in his body bucks against the prospect of this death. He sweats like drops of blood in anguish at the very thought of it.

And he lays his own will down.

He refuses to allow his bodily discomfort and fear win out.

In what follows, we see that he takes the very next steps he prescribes as the requirement for being his disciple in Matthew 16:24. He takes up his cross and carries it with the help of Simon the Cyrene to the place of the skull to be crucified. He lays his life—his perfect, sinless, loving, merciful, gracious life—down for you and for me.

Remember, this isn't your neighbor Randy who dies. It is the very Son of God. He is a gift of love from God for you. He is the offering God makes on your behalf to settle your account forever. God is perfectly just in that the penalty for disobedience is death and he is perfectly loving by providing a payment for you in Jesus. And what does God ask in return? That you let him make you more like his Son than you are now. We'll get into why he does it in a few chapters, but don't miss that imitating Christ isn't about being obedient, though that's a nice target. Christlikeness isn't about holiness, though that will come in time.

What does that mean for Christians?

The Blueprint of Grace

If God's plan for my life is to make it more like Christ's, we see here how that happens. Jesus not only shows us the blueprint but presents himself as the flesh and blood example to follow.

You are most like Christ when you deny yourself and take up your cross and follow him.

6

The First Steps of Faith

Not that I have already obtained this or am already perfect, but I press on to make it my own, because Christ Jesus has made me his own. Brothers, I do not consider that I have made it my own. But one thing I do: forgetting what lies behind and straining forward to what lies ahead, I press on toward the goal for the prize of the upward call of God in Christ Jesus.

—PHILIPPIANS 3:12–14

WHEN I WAS PLAYING baseball in high school and then in college, something trendy to do was to scribe an inspirational quote or word onto the underside of the bill of your cap. I remember mine, "PTMSTWDITTFS." Awe-inspiring, isn't it? It just rolls off the tongue. Try it.

To be honest, guys I played with would ask me all the time what in the world those letters meant; certain they were gibberish. The problem was that the quote I wanted to put on my hat was far too long to write out on the underside of the bill of my hat. "Perhaps the most successful thing we do is take the first step." It's

The Blueprint of Grace

from Dr. K. Bradford Brown. I heard it once. I have no idea who this Dr. Brown was or is, nor the context of quote, but something about it is a bit compelling, isn't it?

For years I was a shy kid, then a shy teenager, then a shy adult. Some people who have known me for a long time find that impossible to believe, but it's true. *Shy* isn't really the word though; I used to be timid. Is it possible to be a timid extrovert? If it is, I was. Anyway, insecurity wracked my psyche for years because I knew I wasn't the person that I should be, nor the person everyone else thought I was. It's hard to put it into words that make a lot of sense because it was, and in many ways still is, a neurosis with which I struggle. That insecurity led me to be fearful of being called a fraud or a hypocrite. It paralyzed me.

And that's the thing about Dr. Brown's words. Wherever I saw them, they hit me as deeply profound. Defining success changes the scorecard. Take a baby step toward a goal? That's success. It doesn't have to be big. And that's the point of the quote. Overcoming the inertia of being stationary and inching toward something you desire is achievement. Have you reached the goal? Only you can know that, but sometimes the most successful thing you do is take the first step. For the alcoholic fighting the addiction, simply driving past the bar and not stopping in for a pint is success. From the outside, you don't know how hard that might be and so you might not even notice it. But for the guy whose marriage is on his last leg because of his drinking, who desperately wants to save his marriage but also craves the mind-numbing effect of alcohol, not stopping even one time is a miracle.

Success can be fickle and it can be fleeting and it can be hard, because success takes work.

So for years, success for me was taking that step toward a goal, often overcoming overwhelming fear and timidity to try and do bold things. I'd love to tell you it's been easy. It hasn't, though. In fact, moving toward a goal, particularly any worthwhile goal, is crazy hard. It feels like an uphill struggle because you have to overcome the inertia that sometimes keeps you from gaining ground, sometimes from a standstill and sometimes from working in the opposite direction of the goal.

This is probably one of the single hardest things about being a Christian—pursuing a holy and godly life. Scripture is chock-full of exhortations to live a life worthy of being called one of God's children. God himself says, "Be holy, for I the LORD your God am holy," multiple times. In the middle of the Sermon on the Mount, an entire sermon on what righteousness looks like, Jesus says, "You therefore must be perfect, as your heavenly Father is perfect" (Matt 5:48). Perfect? Holy? That sounds hard. Where do you even begin?

With the first step of course.

The first step to turning toward God is turning away from sin.

No matter how hard you try, you can't get away from the fact that salvation from your sins is entirely a work of God. Once God has done that work and opened your eyes to the reality that you're a sinner in need of redemption and that redemption is found in Jesus, your only path forward is to seek his face and trust him. That's what we call putting our faith in Christ. Subsequently, repentance is the first fruit of that faith, the first byproduct, if you will.

Let me explain.

God and sin are in opposite directions. They're like negative infinity and infinity, eternally far apart. If you're looking for sin, you can't be looking for God, and vice versa. So it makes sense that the very first thing you would do as you search for redemption would be to stop looking for it in places where it cannot be found. One addicted to gambling doesn't break the habit by continuing to frequent the casino. Redemption isn't found in the midst of the sin. It is wholly elsewhere.

In order to receive the work God has done on your behalf at the cross, you need only see your need of it and accept it, but to do so means forsaking whatever else is going on in your life. As I noted in the previous chapter, you have to leave behind who you have been to become who God wants you to be. In his letter to the

The Blueprint of Grace

Colossians, Paul describes the method to departing from your old ways: "*If* then you have been raised with Christ, seek the things that are above, where Christ is, seated at the right hand of God" (Col 3:1, emphasis added). If that feels a bit vague, Paul makes sure he provides clarity. If you are saved, then live like it and that starts by having your eyes and minds fixed in the right place. "Set your minds on things that are above, not on things that are on earth" (Col 3:2.) It starts with a change of mentality. "Do not be conformed to this world, but be transformed by the *renewal of your mind*, that by testing you may discern what is the will of God, what is good and acceptable and perfect" (Rom 12:2, emphasis added). Success doesn't come from changing your behavior, though that's an outflow. Success comes from changing how you think about your behavior. Success comes by allowing the work that God has done in your inner being, regenerating it and making it new, to push through all your old junk and garbage to create a life that looks different.

God changes your inner self and your outer self is renewed because of it. Paul stresses that rather than trying to adjust your activity, tethering your mind and heart to the things above fuels transformation. Paul continues in Colossians 3, describing a part of what that entails:

> Put to death therefore what is earthly in you: sexual immorality, impurity, passion, evil desire, and covetousness, which is idolatry. On account of these the wrath of God is coming. In these you too once walked, when you were living in them. But now you must put them all away: anger, wrath, malice, slander, and obscene talk from your mouth. Do not lie to one another, seeing that you have put off the old self with its practices and have put on the new self, which is being renewed in knowledge after the image of its creator. (Col 3:5–10)

There's a troublesome thing in the midst of this though. Paul warns the Galatians, "Are you so foolish? Having begun by the Spirit, are you now being perfected by the flesh?" (Gal 3:3) This activity of putting our former self to death is not what brings you closer to God. It can prove to be quite the opposite. To call yourself a Christian because you are putting to death all that is earthly in you inverts the truth. In fact, just prior to the aforementioned verses in Colossians, Paul warns that the practice of self-denial and trying to live your way to salvation looks like wisdom, but has no saving power and no power to transform the heart. It is your relationship with God through Christ that brings you to a new life, not your own deeds.

So what do we do with that information? Human beings are by nature doers, so how do we read the seemingly paradoxical teachings of resting in the work of Christ and putting on our new selves?

If the work of Jesus on the cross establishes a right standing between us and God, then we give ourselves entirely to that truth. How? By doing the thing that Jesus commands: denying ourselves and taking up our cross to follow him. That means turning away from the paths we once trod. Again, God and sin are in opposite directions, so to follow Jesus is to leave behind sinful behavior.

The early church, which was initially comprised of Jews, provides us a good example of some first steps. As they heard that Gentiles were receiving the Holy Spirit through the ministry of Paul and Barnabas, they got together to talk about what was necessary to be a Christian. The question: What parts of Jewish tradition and law were valuable for those who had grown up adhering to it? Ultimately, the list was short. "For it has seemed good to the Holy Spirit and to us to lay on you no greater burden than these requirements: that you abstain from what has been sacrificed to idols, and from blood, and from what has been strangled, and from sexual immorality. If you keep yourselves from these, you will do well" (Acts 15:28–29). Notice the last sentence, "If you keep yourselves from there, *you will do well.*" Did the Gentiles know why? The gathering of Christian leaders, called the Jerusalem Council, didn't explain why these things were good. They simply said that they were. Now that might not seem like much, but it was enough.

How much depth about what the Bible teaches do you need to know to discern what is a sin and what isn't a sin? If you flip

The Blueprint of Grace

back through the Old Testament to read the story of the prophet Jonah, you will find an answer.

Maybe you know the story of Jonah. If you're a Christian or grew up in church, you have probably heard about this prophet who was called to go to a dangerous and pagan place called Ninevah, one of the largest cities of the day, to deliver a message of God's judgment upon them for their behavior. You might think that the message God sent Jonah with was a laundry list of their sins. But it was much shorter than that. "Yet forty days, and Nineveh shall be overthrown!" (Jonah 3:4).

That's it. No explanation of why, no description of what they had done wrong, no encouragement to change their ways. Just a warning that the city was about to be decimated.

Is that enough?

Apparently it is.

> And the people of Nineveh believed God. They called for a fast and put on sackcloth, from the greatest of them to the least of them. The word reached the king of Nineveh, and he arose from his throne, removed his robe, covered himself with sackcloth, and sat in ashes. And he issued a proclamation and published through Nineveh, "By the decree of the king and his nobles: Let neither man nor beast, herd nor flock, taste anything. Let them not feed or drink water, but let man and beast be covered with sackcloth, and let them call out mightily to God. Let everyone turn from his evil way and from the violence that is in his hands. Who knows? God may turn and relent and turn from his fierce anger, so that we may not perish." (Jonah 3:5–10)[1]

You can absolutely turn away from the things that God says are evil without knowing why. There are laws against murder and stealing in every country in the world. God has embedded a sense of right and wrong in every human being and people sometimes fudge those lines for their own convenience or pleasure, but deep down we know there is an appropriate way to live. To cast aside inappropriate behavior, one need only make a conscious choice to do so. As we've already covered though, that decision does not

The First Steps of Faith

equate to being right with God. You can modify your behavior all you want, but changing your heart is the only way that you find yourself justified before God. And the only one who can change your heart is God himself.

So then what? Well, back to the question at hand: What do you actually *do* about what God has done in your heart?

You start by focusing on Jesus and his work at the cross. You begin at the beginning and, to be honest, you don't move on from that. You never budge from the gospel. In a 2019 sermon, John Piper said, "You never outgrow your need for the gospel. You never graduate to a course where the gospel should not be the center of the curriculum. There's no post-gospel graduate school in the Christian life. The center of every ongoing growth in knowledge has Christ crucified, risen, received by faith alone like a little child at the center of the curriculum."[1] You constantly circle and spiral deeper into understanding how the death, burial, and resurrection of Jesus impacts your life.

As you grow in your knowledge and understanding of Jesus and his sacrifice for you, your behavior changes not because you know the sins to avoid, but because you are following Jesus. Your eyes are becoming more and more fixed on him and all the rest of the distractions and temptations in life dwindle in their sway over you. Your singular focus becomes fixed upon the one who died for you.

In the meantime, you take baby steps toward him. You set aside your old behaviors because he tells you they have no part in following him. In time, you figure out why and you learn more about your own inability to live righteously, but the first step is to change your behavior while you learn. You keep yourself from things that keep you away from Christ.

Are there things that get to stay? Sure there are, but only if they serve the purpose God designed for you. They get repurposed into something else. Maybe you've been serving at a homeless

---

1. Piper, "We Will Never Outgrow the Gospel," https://www.desiringgod.org/messages/receive-with-meekness-the-implanted-word/excerpts/we-will-never-outgrow-the-gospel.

The Blueprint of Grace

shelter or food pantry, or perhaps as a foster parent or caregiver for someone developmentally disabled or an aging parent. Those things are well and good and they can serve the kingdom of God and his purposes for your life. That's not to say they absolutely get to remain, because they can be idols in your life, obstacles to actually becoming the person God is calling you to be. So those things are held with an open hand. God may or may not want you to keep doing them. I cannot tell you what you are supposed to be doing in every example.

But Scripture very specifically lists things that are not in the interest of God: malice, wrath, sexual immorality, jealously, covetousness, slander, obscene talk, sorcery, rivalries, dissension, disunity, and division among Christians, drunkenness, and many, many others. Be sure that God is calling you as a believer to leave these behind you. ". . . put off your old self, which belongs to your former manner of life and is corrupt through deceitful desires, and to be renewed in the spirit of your minds, and to put on the new self, created after the likeness of God in true righteousness and holiness" (Eph 4:22–24).

It's the second part of those three verses to which we now turn.

7

Putting On the New

Growing in Obedience

Therefore, if anyone is in Christ, he is a new creation. The old has passed away; behold, the new has come.

—2 Corinthians 5:17

Back in 2017, my wife and I moved to Iowa. Our house had a steep incline in the front yard that dropped down to street level. I'm not entirely sure I could tell you the grade, but it was probably thirty to forty degrees. In a triangle, that might not seem like much, but for a grassy slope that needs mowing every week, it is ridiculous.

When my family first moved into the house, we tried using our trusty Honda push mower, but we couldn't keep the deck flat against the slope from above and we couldn't push up the slope well enough from below. Mowing sideways was possible, but not entirely safe either as the slope was steep enough to cause the mower to tip sideways. For two and a half years, we ran a battery-powered string trimmer over it. It took us roughly thirty minutes to do it. Then one day my wife had an idea. She wanted to turn our front bank into a bed for native prairie plants, specifically flowers and grasses. So, we sprayed the grass with with some weed and grass killer, scattered a wildflower and grass seed blend, covered it with some anti-erosion landscape netting, and waited.

And waited.

We had our concerns the first year. Many plants popped up, but not the ones we had planted. Ground cover weeds like black medick thrived now that the grass was gone. What we found out, interestingly enough, was that the anti-erosion netting, made from biodegradable coconut straw, actually prevented the new shoots from coming up. We had to go through and cut holes, actually tearing back portions of said netting in order to allow the plants to grow. It was frustrating.

Eventually that first year, we had a few varieties of plants that came up, most of which we knew wouldn't bloom that season because they were establishing their root systems. But we were pleasantly surprised to have lupine, black-eyed Susans, goldenrod, bearded beggarticks, purple coneflower, yarrow, prairie mimosa, Maximillian sunflower, evening primrose, sage, fleabane, and several others that we couldn't identify growing in the first year.

Year two was different. Not only did we have lots of plants, but we had an overflowing number of them. We still had some spots where we had to peel back the netting we had put down the first season, but mostly this wild tangle of flora was thriving.

When you become a Christian and you start laying the foundations of living out your faith, it can be a lot like those initial steps. Just like we had to use a grass and weed killer at the beginning of the project, you have to clear out the old first, like I told you about in the previous chapter. But then, once the proverbial ground has been cleared, you're ready to start sowing seed.

Following Christ means investing in your growth as a follower of Christ.

When God regenerates your heart by the power of the Holy Spirit, you may be a new person, but you've got a lot to learn. In the apostle Peter's first letter, he describes the state of man thusly: "Like newborn infants, long for the pure spiritual milk, that by it you may grow up into salvation—if indeed you have tasted that the Lord is good" (1 Pet 2:2–3). When you're born again, you experience something profound, infancy. When you're an infant, you have no idea that you're helpless; you just know that your belly is empty or you're tired or you need a diaper changed. You don't have the words for it, so what do you do? You cry. You have needs and you communicate that you have needs by wailing until those needs are met.

When you surrender your life into God's hands, you are very much so like a baby. The difference is that you can communicate your needs more clearly. And you know, one of the first things we know about repentance is that you need to tell someone about it and then make a declaration that you're going to follow Jesus.

When Peter delivered his explanation about what had happened on the day of Pentecost, people were shocked. They asked him what they needed to do about what they had done, which was reject Jesus. The people gathered in Jerusalem were there after the Passover celebration, after the crucifixion, after the resurrection. They were part of the crowds that had turned on Jesus, from one minute welcoming him into the city with shouts of, "Hosanna to the Son of David! Blessed is he who comes in the name of the Lord! Hosanna in the highest! (Matt 21:9)," to shouting, "Let him be crucified!" (Matt 27:22). These folks, this mob, they were "cut to the heart," as the text of Acts 2:37 tells us, and felt the need to do something in response. Peter tells them to repent and be baptized in the name of Jesus, to not just turn from their rejection of Christ but to publicly align with him by being baptized in his name.

Truthfully, repentance is the first fruit of faith. It's the very first step someone convicted about their sin takes. That should be followed by proclaiming what Christ has done on your behalf through baptism. There is a lot of teaching about baptism, what it is and what it isn't. Baptism has no saving power. It does not impart grace. It does not guarantee salvation. It is the believer's public declaration that they believe that Christ died for their sins, was

The Blueprint of Grace

buried, and was then resurrected on the third day in accordance with the Scriptures. It is an act that signifies, by its nature, the putting to death the old life and being raised to new life in Christ.

Is that all that happens in the life of a Christian?

One repents from their sins and gets baptized to tell the watching world what they believe to be true and that's the end of it?

Seems off, doesn't it.

Because there is so much more in the Bible than just that. There are laws and stories and prayers and poems and instructions and promises, and if we only have all of those for what, a ceremonial act of remembrance that takes all of ten seconds to do, that feels pretty useless to me.

Like I said, repentance and baptism are first steps, not last steps. Being a Christian is a life-long pursuit. The apostle Paul likens it to a race from time to time. It's not a hundred-meter dash or the steeplechase or even a marathon. It's a race that begins when you accept Christ's free gift of forgiveness and ends when you die.

That is, hopefully, a long, long time, decades even. How are you to live then?

Now that's the question with which every Christian struggles.

But in some ways it's a silly struggle. We know what to do. We have a book that tells us all about it. In Peter's second letter, he gives some really practical instruction:

> His divine power has granted to us all things that pertain to life and godliness, through the knowledge of him who called us to his own glory and excellence, by which he has granted to us his precious and very great promises, so that through them you may become partakers of the divine nature, having escaped from the corruption that is in the world because of sinful desire. For this very reason, make every effort to supplement your faith with virtue, and virtue with knowledge, and knowledge with self-control, and self-control with steadfastness, and steadfastness with godliness, and godliness with brotherly affection, and brotherly affection with love. For if these qualities are yours and are increasing, they keep

you from being ineffective or unfruitful in the knowledge of our Lord Jesus Christ. (2 Pet 1:3–8)

Notice what he writes. Firstly, God has given us everything we need to know about life and godliness, and that has come through what we know about Jesus, and through Jesus you and I become partakers in the "divine nature," that is, we receive salvation from our sins. So if you're a Christian, God has given you everything you need to know about what it means to exist as a Christian in the day in, day out of your life. The command "be holy, for I the LORD your God am holy" (Lev 19:2) dates back to the Old Testament but still applies today. The standard has never changed.

But then Peter shifts from this theological truth to an extremely practical list of spiritual supplements: "faith with virtue, and virtue with knowledge, and knowledge with self-control, and self-control with steadfastness, and steadfastness with godliness, and godliness with brotherly affection, and brotherly affection with love." Now, there are some pretty churchy words there, and I'll explain them here in just a minute, but notice that this list builds upon itself. Peter describes the pattern of growth as one of supplementing faith. What is a supplement? It's something that adds to something else. If, for example, you were reading *The Scarlet Letter* by Nathaniel Hawthorne in your American literature class, your teacher may assign some parallel reading from an American history textbook or perhaps writings by various Puritan authors like Jonathan Edwards or Cotton Mather in an effort to supplement your understanding of the text.

Peter suggests a list of attitudes and traits as supplements meant to strengthen and bolster your faith, to make help it stand up under pressure.

So what are these supplements and how do they help? Let me try and quickly explain them because one could probably write an entire chapter about each one of them.

When you come to faith, you begin to shun unrighteousness. That inherently means that you're going to turn to virtue, a moral excellence. Straighten up and fly right. Look, that's something that the Holy Spirit empowers in our life as we begin to rightly understand sin and redemption and grace and the cross, which comes through, guess what, knowledge. We throw ourselves into the Bible and suddenly we realize that this is not quite as easy as we thought it was going to be; not because doing the right thing is hard, but because the wrong thing is *always* right there for us to choose. What do we need? Self control! Imagine that.

You can see how the list progresses: "self-control with steadfastness"—that's faithfulness, continually choosing. "Faithfulness with godliness"—that's developing Godly character, which is different than virtue, which is the right action; and while you can do the right thing for the wrong reasons, godliness is having the right heart. Brotherly affection comes as we begin to see everyone else's needs. We begin to actually like the people around us for who they are and who God designed them to be and finally we take that brotherly affection and cap it with love: acting on behalf of others, serving them, sacrificing ourselves for their benefit and good.

And then to cap all that off, Peter writes that if these qualities are present in your life and character, they produce a fruitful life.

Therein lies the rub.

This stuff doesn't flow out of you naturally, even after you're saved. It is work. The Bible tells us lots of things to not do. It's a list from which you can probably quickly fire off about ten answers. But we also have a to-do list encapsulated by the Greatest Commandment, found in Matthew, Mark, and Luke: "Love the Lord your God . . . and love your neighbor as your self." The Bible says a lot about what being a Christian looks like in real-time rather than just theory. It is not as simple as creating a punch list of Christian duty, however, because checking things off your holy to-do list doesn't gain you favor with God. You don't become more saved. You don't mark things off the list in order to score points or to make yourself look good. You do it because it makes God look good. It shows the people around you that you think God is pretty nifty and worthy of your praise and worship and, therefore, your obedience.

So you must choose these things.

You have to choose to grow. You have to decide to become more like the person God wants you to be rather than the person you are right now. Every day you are faced with an infinite number of decisions and each one is an opportunity to either honor God or dishonor God. Yes, that means picking out your socks in the morning, too. The easy way to honor God when you pick out your socks in the morning is to recognize him as the provider of them. You could not have socks. You could not have the money to buy a pair. God, in his wisdom and providence, made cotton, and he knew how it would be used to cushion and warm our feet. So go ahead and thank God for the blessing of socks. It's a tiny blessing, but you never know how much you like your socks until you don't have a pair.

The next thing you know, as you choose to learn more, grow more, trust more, let go of your own preconceived notion of growth more, your life starts taking shape. You begin to see more clearly why God asks you to live differently than the world around you. You have a new lens to help you to view the world in all of its splendor and trouble. You find yourself rejecting unbiblical attitudes and behaviors.

Here is the best part: God's way is the best way. God didn't arbitrarily decide what is right and wrong. He designed and created the world for human flourishing, for the best experience a man or woman could possibly have.

Can you imagine what this world would be like if people valued one another as God values them? What would your community look like if everyone saw everyone else as being made in the image of God? Would there be murder? Would there be abuse? I know that may sound and feel reductionistic, distilling down complex societal problems down into a single source, but is it true? If we all looked after one another as God would intend us to, every man, woman, child, parent, grandparent, uncle, boss, employee, mayor, president—you name it—the world would look like a drastically different place.

If someone is poor and struggling, who stands in the gap to provide? If everyone trusted in God for their provision, anyone—*everyone*—could meet such a need without fear of being taken advantage of by someone else. Altruism, real and genuine self-sacrificial service of others, not only becomes possible, but it is fully realized as we see the dignity of every person and serve them rather than seek to protect our own bottom line.

What about governance? Who decides what should be permissible in the public sphere? If we are all pursuing God's standard of behavior, if we have all submitted ourselves to see one another as valuable as coequals in God's eyes, then the laws we pass protect will everyone regardless of age, gender, ethnicity, and the like.

Let's get a little bit more personal.

Consider marriage. Scripture calls marriage a covenant relationship between a man and a woman that reflects the relationship between Christ and the church. Now consider the biology of human beings. We cannot reproduce ourselves. Our genetic code is divided between a man and a woman and can only be reproduced by the joining of one man and one woman. The foundation of procreation is one in that requires the connection of two people. If you consider the brain science of the act of reproduction, you find that the hormones released into the body during intercourse, endorphins and oxytocin, change the chemistry of the brain to create an intense bond through the physical act. By its very nature, sex connects those involved through processes over which the individual has no control. This is why God intended sexual relations to be for a man and a woman in the covenant bounds of marriage, a lifelong commitment to serving one another.

Imagine the safety and security found when a husband and wife, who are complete novices in physical intimacy, choose to learn how to serve one another, to please one another in the bedroom. They make the conscience choice to look out for one another in this most precious and vulnerable moment and spend the rest of their lives committed to one another, learning likes and dislikes in an effort to make sure that the other person feels valued and loved. There's no selfishness that leads to abuse and rape. There are no perversions or fantasies of another person because the desire is to love and serve the one to whom you have bonded yourself "'til death do you part."

I find it compelling to think through this most intimate of relationships when I consider how deeply our transformation should run. You can playact the Christian life, but that does not lead to actual growth. God will produce the growth in you as you seek to rely less on your own strength and understanding and trust more in his.

This is what Paul writes about in Romans 12:2, "Do not be conformed to this world, but be transformed by the renewal of your mind, that by testing you may discern what is the will of God, what is good and acceptable and perfect." Knowing what God wants and why God wants it helps you live a life that reflects what God wants. You may start off that journey not knowing the why, but in time, if you're seeking to grow closer to God through the study of his Word, letting that study drive how you behave, and developing relationships with others who are trying to grow closer to him, God's character begins to make more sense. Not perfect sense, mind you, as neither you nor I will ever quite understand God like God understands us, but we don't need perfect understanding in order to reflect God's goodness and holiness in our lives.

That's what it means to grow in Christlikeness, to become more of who God wants us to be.

Of course, even as we grow closer to God and so develop a more Christlike worldview and perspective, we're still not going to get it right every time.

So then what happens?

8

The Unexpected Uh-Ohs

If we say we have no sin, we deceive ourselves, and the truth is not in us. If we confess our sins, he is faithful and just to forgive us our sins and to cleanse us from all unrighteousness. If we say we have not sinned, we make him a liar, and his word is not in us.

—1 John 1:8–10

When I was a kid, my family would pile into our van to go on vacation to visit dear friends some four hours away in Central Illinois. If it was autumn, my nose would invariably bleed profusely. My parents and doctor didn't figure it out until much later in life, but it turns out I have overwhelming seasonal allergies. I had always thought I was susceptible to pink eye, but it turns out I was simply allergic to grass pollen. I'll never forget being on a baseball field and having my eyes water and itch and burn and swell so badly that I had to be taken out of the game because I could not see through the gunk and tears. It was awful.

The Unexpected Uh-Ohs

Over the years I've undergone various over-the-counter and prescriptive remedies. I have employed eye drops, nasal inhalers, shots, and umpteen different varieties of antihistamines to stem the tide of the reactions to these environmental irritants. They worked, sort of. If I was caught without or if the effects of the medicine wore off midday, I was in trouble.

One such occurrence took place in mid-to-late May of 1999. I was sitting lakeside at a youth camp and my twelve-hour dosage of fexofenadine HCL metabolized out of my system about three and a half hours before my next dosage was due. My eyes were swollen nearly shut within minutes and I had to have a friend escort me to the nurses' station because my eyes burned so badly that I could not open them. I walked in and someone gave me a mirror. I looked like I had been in a prize fight, puffy and blotchy and discolored. I was caught completely off guard by the reaction. I was given a fast-acting dose of diphenhydramine and kept in the office overnight for observation. The following morning they shipped me to town to get a corticosteroid injection and, somewhat miraculously, I didn't have a reaction like that the rest of the summer, though there were still a few days of mild symptoms.

I still have seasonal allergies. They're not nearly as hard on me as they were when I was a child, but come mid-April nosebleeds, watery eyes, sneezes, and constant nasal drip become part of my everyday existence. They come and go. There are good days and bad days and I know that I am going to have them. I have a regular maintenance dose of medication that I take year-round to help the situation.

But what would happen if I woke up tomorrow and announced I was cured? What if when my eyes opened in the morning, I said, "I'm cured! I have taken my last ten-milligram dose of montelukast. I'll never have to deal with seasonal allergies again because I took one dose of this miraculous medicine"? How would that turn out?

I imagine that when mid-April hit, I would likely get the sniffles. My eyes would start to get "gritchy," as my wife and I like to say. I might even have a nosebleed. What then? Would I reconsider my condition? Would I think about medicating? Or would I stick to my guns, confident I was no longer affected by seasonal allergies? Or was I wrong?

I don't expect to not have to take allergy meds this side of heaven. It's a condition I manage the best that I can, but even then I sometimes get caught out. Occasionally, the pollen count is higher than my body can handle, even when I've been cautious and diligent in my regimen.

Why?

Because I have a body that sometimes doesn't react well to the air around me. I would love to not have to think about it. I would love to be free from it, but I'm not. At least not yet.

Likewise, I have a sin problem.

It's inconvenient. It's bothersome. It frustrates me to no end. I take steps to prepare myself. Yet even then, I fall to temptation. Every single human being does. If we could will ourselves out of it, I think some would. That's the problem with sin though, isn't it? The fact that I even have to say "some would" implies that most of us wouldn't—at least not in every instance, not permanently, not eternally. In his *Confessions*, Augustine writes, "Oh, Master, make me chase and celibate—but not yet!" (*Confessions* 8.7). I can hear the cry of desperation in these words, words that echo those of the apostle Paul, "Wretched man that I am! Who will deliver me from this body of death?" (Rom 7:24).

There is in every human being a desire to set his or her own course, to engage and indulge in whatever will bring prosperity or peace or joy or pleasure or security. To the detriment of our own souls, we choose to pursue that which brings the greatest benefit for us in the now.

Yet in the Bible, God's message is clear: "You shall be holy, for I the LORD your God am holy" (Lev 19:2). God desires those whom he calls his own to look and act how he wants them to act. There is a standard of behavior to which a Christian is held, even if they cannot always meet it. I have read several parenting books that talk about how high-functioning families have their own code of ethics so that when a child needs to be disciplined, the parent can say to him or her, "That's not who you are as a Jones. That's not what being a Jones is about." The parent teaches the child what it means to be a member of the family and then holds that child accountable to that model.

So what happens when someone strays away from appropriate behavior? What happens when a Christian, who should know better, sins?

Repentance is a lifetime pursuit that demonstrates continued trust in Christ's death on your behalf.

There are some passages in the Bible that stir me deeply. They resonate with something deep in my heart that causes my eyes to well up with tears (not because of the pollen this time). The apostle John, the elder statesmen of the first-century church, wrote letters to the church and his very first one, 1 John, begins with a beautiful description of God: "This is the message we have heard from him and proclaim to you, that God is light, and in him is no darkness at all" (1:5). Can you imagine that? Can you fathom what it means that "God is light, and in him is no darkness at all"? Darkness is literally the absence of light. So can darkness and light coexist? No! Physically and scientifically, such a phenomenon is impossible. As God is perfect, there is no sin in him, and because there is no sin in him, he cannot be in the presence of sin. As light and dark cannot be in the same place at the same time, so God and sin cannot be in the same place at the same time.

But you know, it's not that description of God that stirs me. It's not even the next few verses, though they are moving.

> If we say we have fellowship with him while we walk in darkness, we lie and do not practice the truth. But if we walk in the light, as he is in the light, we have fellowship with one another, and the blood of Jesus his Son cleanses us from all sin. If we say we have no sin, we deceive ourselves, and the truth is not in us. If we confess our sins, he is faithful and just to forgive us our sins and to cleanse us from all unrighteousness. If we

say we have not sinned, we make him a liar, and his word is not in us. (1 John 1:6–10)

We cannot have fellowship with God *and* pursue sin. The only fellowship we have with God is when we are walking in light rather than darkness. John writes that we must own the fact that we're sinners, and when we do own it and fess up to our sins, God forgives us and cleanses us from all of our unrighteousness. What a beautiful sentiment. And that matters because a saved person sins.

That feels so wrong to write. I hate that saved people sin. Not every sin is scandalous and public, like an affair or a homicide. Some are innocuous: a lingering glance, an idleness, a half-truth, a careless word of critique or anger, or stealing time at work focusing on something other than your job. Nobody lives perfectly. We are expected to, but in truth nobody actually does.

That's why God sent Jesus, isn't it? If we were able to do it perfectly, Jesus wouldn't have to had to come and rescue us. But we can't do it. That necessitated God doing something about it. And so when we own up to our shortcomings, to the fact that we're in need of intervention by God, when we confess our sins, God is faithful to forgive them and wipe the slate clean with the blood of Jesus. And even that, as beautiful as it is, stands as a reminder of what moves me to the core, which is the very next verse.

1 John 2 begins with these words, "My little children, I am writing these things to you so that you may not sin. But if anyone does sin, we have an advocate with the Father, Jesus Christ the righteous" (2:1). John writes to remind Christians about the nature of God and of sin and how the two, like oil and water, don't mix, because he wants his friends, his children, those who are young in their faith, to understand how important it is to walk in the light rather than darkness, to get a sense that sin isn't going away unless you put it away. In short, he writes what he writes because he wants the people who will receive the letter to stay away from sin.

And that is beautiful. A pastor telling his congregation the truth about themselves so they can know how to live according to God's will is a beautiful thing.

But . . .

The Unexpected Uh-Ohs

John knows the reality as well. "But if anyone does sin . . ." It's going to happen. It's inevitable. This is where my heart swells with regret and pain. I have sinned. I know exactly what this man is writing about. I know not to sin, and yet I sin. So the rest of the verse breaks me apart inside. "But if anyone does sin, we have an advocate with the Father, Jesus Christ the righteous." Right now, Jesus is at the right hand of the Father, interceding and advocating for his people.

And what does that look like? When you sin, I think the conversation between Father and Son looks something like this:

> *Jesus*: OK, Father, you saw what Bill just did there. I saw it too. You and I both know Bill shouldn't have been doing that. Bill knows he shouldn't have done that either. But Father, look at this . . . (*Jesus turns his back to God, showing him the scars from where the cat-o'-nine-tails tore at his flesh; then he turns and holds out his wrists to show where the nails that held him to the cross were driven through; then lifts his garment to reveal the hole in his side where the spear pierced him; then points to the scars on his forehead from the crown of thorns the Romans pressed onto his brow.*) Father, I've already paid the penalty for Bill's sin. It did all of this (*gesturing to himself*) so that Bill's debt for his sin would be forgiven, so that you would remember my death rather than sentence him to his. I already died for Bill's sin, Father. Forgive him.

Sin can feel like this huge, derailing influence. It *is* a huge, derailing influence. It rears its ugly head at the most inopportune times. A person's sinful nature sits just beneath the surface, waiting to be uncovered. It's like the volcano waiting to erupt; sometimes it can feel long dormant, but you're never more than a moment away from committing a sin. God told Adam and Eve's firstborn son, Cain, that "sin is crouching at the door. Its desire is contrary to you, but you must rule over it" (Gen 4:7). If you give it an inch, it will take a lightyear.

Often, Christians merely try to avoid temptation. They stay away from situations that they know will prick their interests. But the problem is everywhere. It is not a fixed set of circumstances that draws sinful behavior out of a person, but the person themselves who makes everything into temptation.

And that can feel utterly overwhelming.

Such is the life of a Christian.

This is why we're called to deny ourselves and take up our cross. It's a daily decision to crucify the flesh so that God's Spirit can live in and through us.

The opportunity to sin surrounds us. God has given us what we need to know to identify it and so avoid it, but he also has given us victory over it through Jesus. We have someone in our corner who advocates for us and promises to forgive and change us because he loves us.

So, even though I know, I deeply believe, that I have been forgiven of my sins, I still sin. I still struggle. I still need Jesus. I still need the gospel. Every. Stinking. Day.

I still need Jesus to make me into someone different, someone more like him.

And he does it through his body, the church.

9

Building Up the Body (Part I)
The Life of the Church

> As you come to him, a living stone rejected by men but in the sight of God chosen and precious, you yourselves like living stones are being built up as a spiritual house, to be a holy priesthood, to offer spiritual sacrifices acceptable to God through Jesus Christ... But you are a chosen race, a royal priesthood, a holy nation, a people for his own possession, that you may proclaim the excellencies of him who called you out of darkness into his marvelous light.
>
> —1 Peter 2:4–5, 9

TOGETHER EVERYONE ACHIEVES MORE. Maybe you've heard that before. It's an acronym that spells "team." As a former college athlete, the idea of being a teammate means something.

I attended a NCAA Division III school where there were no athletic scholarships. As such, most of my teammates weren't there to play baseball but to pursue a degree. That isn't to say they weren't dedicated to the game, but a drive for suitable employment following graduation fueled their motivation for attending the school. Our practice schedule during the week was often tempered by the demands of the academic rigors of the school. So it would be common for a player to show up, field some grounders or shag some flies during batting practice, take a few swings of their own, handle their conditioning on their own time, and be released so they could go take care of the real reason they were at the school.

I was no different. Most of the time I would come and get my work in and not spare a second thought to how I could be helping the team get better. As a pitcher, I would come to practice just to get my own work in. I would do my conditioning work, throw my bullpen session, and then be dismissed from practice so I could go do the academic work that allowed me to stay on the team. It was a balance between being selfish and selfless. At times I was the former and at others the latter. In other ways, I was a good teammate. I shared what I knew about pitching with other pitchers. We constantly talked about how to get more movement on our sinker and how to help each other better disguise whatever pitch we were throwing. I carried a catcher's mitt in my bag because I was always donning a mask and shin guards to catch my fellow hurlers in the bullpen. I threw batting practice, hit ground balls for the infielders to practice, and filled in wherever else I was asked to fill in. I didn't take much initiative in those things, but if someone asked for help, I was happy to give it.

Even so, baseball is a unique sport.

It's a team game, but it is a massively individual game as well. During practice you prepare for possibilities: you shag flies, you practice throwing on the run, you field hundreds of ground balls, and as a team you learn and practice various situations that may never actually happen during a game. Baseball is incredibly unpredictable. Unless you are a pitcher or catcher, you can go a while without having to make a play. But when the time is right, you're measured by whether or not you're ready to perform. It is vastly different than on a football field or on a basketball court. In those two arenas, you're on all the time. If you don't do your job to the best of your ability every single play, your team faces a high

Building Up the Body (Part I)

probability of failure. It's a higher-stakes proposition. If you fail in these circumstances, the cost is much higher.

So what do you do? Just like the game of baseball, you learn your role. You practice, you drill, you prepare. Then, hopefully, when the time comes, you execute.

That's not just for sports though. Regardless of the field in which you happen to work, this is what training looks like. You have to learn how to be successful in your field. Simple or complex, you are responsible for learning whatever system you are working in and then execute whatever it is that you've learned, whether you're the starting right guard for the Kansas City Chiefs or you're working the register at your local burger joint.

You can attend a sporting event and quickly determine whether or not a team is prepared in the same way that you can visit a new restaurant and tell pretty quickly whether or not they are going to have success. It's obvious. And what is the difference? Often it's a team working together, supporting one another, each member performing his or her role.

Friend, it takes more than you and a Bible to be a successful Christian. That may be a good first step, but the Christian life is not intended to be an entirely individual pursuit.

God equips Christians through the community and ministry of the church.

I don't know when I first considered it, but in the past I had always read the epistles of the New Testament as though they were written to me. In some fashion I suppose they are, but they are specifically written to the church in Rome or Corinth or Thessalonica, to name a few. And beyond the reality that they are written to "the church" in a specific area, I cannot say that I quickly grasped that meant the entire body of believers in that city.

Growing up in St. Louis, I always imagined the letters were written to the church I went to, but also that it was meant for me as an individual. Of course, that's true, but unlike those written to Timothy, Titus, and Philemon, these letters were for an entire

The Blueprint of Grace

community of believers. The context set the message, but also set the application. It's not wrong to read Philippians 1:3 as, "I thank my God in all my remembrance of [*insert your name*]." But it's not exactly what Paul meant. I think Paul would be thankful for individuals. In fact, in his letters he often names plenty of people for whom he is thankful. Yet, his letters are meant for groups of people.

The entire Bible is written for groups of people rather than individuals. You certainly can and should take the Scriptures and seek to apply them in and to your life, but the Bible is far more than just a book of instructions for an individual. It lays out how individuals should function as a body, each one a part of a whole. Much of Paul's writing to these churches scattered around the Mediterranean and Asia Minor consists of how Christians should live in light of the gospel. In each instance, there is a togetherness he emphasizes, a unity that he stresses develops not out of a geographic reality, but the spiritual reality of the gospel; that there is no longer a division between "Greek and Jew, circumcised and uncircumcised, barbarian, Scythian, slave, free; but Christ is all, and in all" (Col 3:11). God created a new humanity through Jesus' atoning work on the cross, a humanity that consists of those redeemed by the blood of the spotless Lamb.

But what are we supposed to do about it? I've mentioned that we're supposed to crave spiritual milk because we're spiritual infants. I've talked about the putting off the old and putting on the new, but one of the most critical aspects of being a Christian is that you're not alone in it.

There are other people who are just as much a sinner as you are, whom God rescued from themselves just as he did you. And throughout Scripture, God tells us that we're to be looking out for each other. The fact that Christians are there to help other Christians is almost foundational to being the church. One of the best passages we get on the subject is found in Paul's letter to Ephesus:

> And he [Christ] gave the apostles, the prophets, the evangelists, the shepherds and teachers, to equip the saints for the work of ministry, for building up the body of Christ, until we all attain to the unity of the faith and

Building Up the Body (Part I)

of the knowledge of the Son of God, to mature manhood, to the measure of the stature of the fullness of Christ, so that we may no longer be children, tossed to and fro by the waves and carried about by every wind of doctrine, by human cunning, by craftiness in deceitful schemes. Rather, speaking the truth in love, we are to grow up in every way into him who is the head, into Christ, from whom the whole body, joined and held together by every joint with which it is equipped, when each part is working properly, makes the body grow so that it builds itself up in love. (Eph 4:11–16)

These words give shape to what should be transpiring in every church around the world. Christ ascends into heaven following his resurrection and when he does, he sends the Holy Spirit to empower Christians to live as they should. He also gives gifts to the church, spiritual gifts, among which are found this fivefold ministry described in verse 11: "the apostles, the prophets, the evangelists, the shepherds and teachers." These five gifts are given to equip the saints for the work of the ministry. In modern contexts, we take these five gifts to be the pastoral gifts that help Christians learn and grow, thus becoming more Christlike. But the goal is to develop not just a Christlike mindset, but a Christlike life.

The gifts are given to equip the saints for the work of the ministry, which is "building up the body of Christ." The church, "the body of Christ," as it is called here, needs to be strengthened, to be built up, edified, pushed toward maturity. I'll come back to what that maturity looks like in just a moment, but take note of this: it is the work of those pastoral gifts to get Christians ready to help other Christians grow and mature into their salvation. Then it's like Paul turns on two big flashing neon signs about what maturity looks like.

Firstly, we have unity: ". . . equip the saints for the work of ministry, for building up the body of Christ, *until* we all attain to the unity of the faith" (Eph 4:12–13, emphasis added). One of the first mark of a mature believer is the commonality of what it means to be a believer. I love what Alistair Begg said in an October 2018 sermon at Midwestern Baptist Theological Seminary:

The Blueprint of Grace

> The communities around us are supposed to be able to come into our local churches and say, "Aha! So this is the difference that Jesus makes." The unifying feature is that we are not a group of people who would all naturally choose to go on vacation with each other . . . The unifying feature is the drama that has taken place in the work of God in Christ among His people . . . What makes a church a church isn't the gathering, the music, the relationships with each other, the Sunday School, the Life groups, the ministry, the Bible, the tithing—No. What makes a church is the gospel.[1]

God doesn't bring Christians together over common interests. In fact, quite the opposite. There were Cardinals and Cubs fans in my former church, Packers and Bears fans, Iowa and Iowa State fans. We don't have things in common, and that in and of itself is the beauty of the gospel. It is for everyone, not just the people who look like you and act like you and grew up in your town and agree that Duran Duran is a criminally underrated band. Christian unity, or gospel-focused unity, if you prefer, centers on the one thing we all have in common: we are sinners who need a Savior and Christ is that Savior. This truth leads us to encourage one another as we remember that we all need support and we all need to be rescued from ourselves. It also causes us to extend grace to one another because we know our own struggles, our own proclivities, our own sins that we try and put to death, and if we are sinners in need of grace and everyone else around us are sinners, they need grace too. So there is unity to be found in facing a common plight, the struggle between our sinful flesh and our renewed spirit, and a common enemy, the devil, who seeks to destroy us. We can and should stand together in our struggle and in our fight because there is strength in numbers, "And though a man might prevail against one who is alone, two will withstand him—a threefold cord is not quickly broken" (Eccl 4:12).

Secondly, Paul draws attention to "knowledge of the son of God." The path of growth consists of learning more about who

---

1. Begg, "Spurgeon Lectures, Part 1."

Building Up the Body (Part I)

God is and what he is about. I cannot count the number of times I have read a passage of Scripture and my elementary understanding, while sufficient at the time, grew into a deeper understanding that ushered me into a stronger reliance on God. It's happening even now, as I am preaching through the book of Colossians at my church. Each time, through the letter I see more nuance and depth that applies to how I live out my faith as a Christian. And the amazing thing is that I learn more about God as I study God's Word with others. I read and study and gain knowledge, but it's when I begin to communicate what I'm learning as I read that I begin to grow. I share the insights I've gained through my study and others share their insights with me. Notice what Paul writes; one of the points of maturing is so "that we may no longer be children, tossed to and fro by the waves and carried about by every wind of doctrine." Maturing in the faith means grasping deeper theology; it means defending what you know to be true; it means standing firm on the Rock of salvation, Jesus Christ. By involving yourself with the body of Christ, the church, you find a space to be taught, encouraged, held accountable, and even rebuked or corrected if it comes to that.

To the Galatians, Paul writes that we are to share one another's burdens. Christ himself commanded such for his people: "A new commandment I give to you, that you love one another: just as I have loved you, you also are to love one another" (John 13:34). As a Christian, you have a responsibility to your fellow Christian to love and serve and support one another.

Not only do you have a responsibility to do so, but to not do so is to handicap the body of Christ. "Rather, speaking the truth in love, we are to grow up in every way into him who is the head, into Christ, from whom the whole body, joined and held together by every joint with which it is equipped, when each part is working properly, makes the body grow so that it builds itself up in love" (Eph 4:15-16). If a part of your body isn't working properly, you would say you have a handicap. This is the language the Bible uses here. Each part of the body, each person, is an integral member of it. All of the members of the body are under the control of the head, or at least they should be. This is why membership matters. We submit to one another's oversight as we are led and shepherded by those Christ gives to the church to equip us: the apostles, prophets, evangelists, pastors, and teachers.

God blesses Christians with the church in order to help them learn to live the life the desires of them, one of development and purpose.

Allowing someone else, either pastor/elder types or members of the congregation in general, to speak truth into your life helps you grow toward maturity.

This maturity looks like not staying where you are when you came to know Christ, but growing in knowledge and trust of the one who called you out of darkness and into light, and so integrating your life into the life of the church.

But it's not just the life of the church with which God is concerned.

It's also the ministry of the church . . .

10

Building Up the Body (Part II)
The Ministry of the Church

Therefore, if anyone is in Christ, he is a new creation. The old has passed away; behold, the new has come. All this is from God, who through Christ reconciled us to himself and gave us the ministry of reconciliation; that is, in Christ God was reconciling the world to himself, not counting their trespasses against them, and entrusting to us the message of reconciliation. Therefore, we are ambassadors for Christ, God making his appeal through us. We implore you on behalf of Christ, be reconciled to God.

—2 Corinthians 5:17–20

I AM FASCINATED BY nonprofit organizations. Some of them make perfect sense to me, and some not so much. For instance, for every OneEighty, an organization in the Quad Cities area of Illinois and Iowa focused on anti-recidivism and addiction counseling that exists to bring hope, love, and opportunity to people and communities impacted by crisis, poverty, and/or addiction, there is the 501st Legion, a group of costumed Star Wars enthusiasts based on the

The Blueprint of Grace

villains of the movie saga, who want to contribute to their community through Star Wars–related events to promote fundraising and volunteerism to show that bad guys can do good. Both have positive ends but work through very different means. As is the case for most nonprofits, there is a unifying cause. The stronger, the bigger, the more foundational, the more recognized the cause, the greater the support.

But even efforts like the 501st Legion are somewhat limited in reach. If you're not a cosplayer, perhaps even if you're not a Star Wars cosplayer, the organization might not be to your liking. There tends to be a drawing in of similar personalities, backgrounds, or interests in a many charitable efforts. Even the consideration of proximity matters. I don't expect people from my hometown of St. Louis to support OneEighty, even though it is a fantastic organization. People in my hometown are more likely to support a local charity focused on similar cultural issues rather than send their money some 250 miles north to the Quad Cities area, where I lived for six years.

Location aside, though, what really brings people to invest and connect with these humanitarian efforts lies in their attempt to tackle real-life hardships. I concede that may feel overgeneralized, that not every "successful" nonprofit fits that mold. However, in my experience, limited in breadth as they may be, charitable organizations with targeted, regionally specific missions garner better community support. There's no single answer as to why that is generally the case, but a direct line can be drawn between an individual's experience and causes said individual will support; that is, there seems to be a correlation between buy-in and personal history. When the struggles are near to you, circumstances you have experienced and wrestled with or problems you have fought through yourself, you are more likely to engage in trying to find or create helpful solutions for others.

People who have suffered with food insecurity are more likely to invest their time, money, and energy in providing it for others. Those who have been homeless remember what it is like to not have a roof overhead and so they are more likely to help those in that very predicament. Those who have broken free from addiction recognize that others are stuck in the cycle and need help, so they become sponsors and counselors. Often, seeing yourself in others as they face down life-altering problems drives you to seek to help. It doesn't always work that way, mind you, but in general, when you can see the need clearly, you more easily get on board with meeting it. People rally around a cause.

Part of my fascination with nonprofits comes from a healthy respect for their mission. As a pastor, I often wonder whether the best strategy is to attempt to engage in trying to find solutions for hunger, addiction, poverty, etc., or to support the local nonprofit that is already doing those things. There are plenty of faith-based organizations that work toward such ends. OneEighty is one such organization.

I think that Christians and churches should get involved in serving their community, but is that what the church is for? After all, former Archbishop of Canterbury William Temple is attributed as saying, "The church is the only cooperative society in the world that exists for the benefit of its non-members." While I agree with that sentiment, I'm not sure that's quite right. As a pastor, I think often about the church where I serve. How are we different from a nonprofit charity? What about the church separates it from the local food bank or women's shelter? What is a church's place in its community? What should be its focus?

The church is more than a nonprofit organization. It is more than a support group. It is more than a group of people who seek to meet the needs of a community. The church is God's chosen vehicle to communicate to the people of the world that he loves them and died for them.

The church is God's missionary force called to display his goodness and mercy to the watching world.

Throughout the Bible, God sets aside people for his purposes. Beginning in the Old Testament, God creates Adam and Eve to represent him, to have dominion over the earth; he chooses Noah to be

The Blueprint of Grace

the man through whom he would deliver mankind from the terrible flood he was about to unleash on the world; he calls Abram to leave his father and mother and everything he knew so that he might make him the father of many nations; he tells Samuel to anoint David as the king to succeed Saul; he selects Solomon to be the one who would build his temple in Jerusalem; he gives Jonah a message for Ninevah, Obadiah a message for Edom, Amos a message for the Northern Kingdom of Israel, and the list goes on and on.

When Jesus redeemed people from every tribe and tongue by his death on the cross, it was not so that each redeemed person could follow after their own way or so that their lives and the lives of those around them could be better in the here and now. In fact, Jesus expressly says otherwise. In the Gospel of John, Jesus explains the opposition that comes from following him: "If the world hates you, know that it has hated me before it hated you . . . If they persecuted me, they will also persecute you" (John 15:18, 20). Then he doubles down on that just a few verses later: "I have said these things to you, that in me you may have peace. In the world you will have tribulation. But take heart; I have overcome the world" (John 16:33). Life actually becomes more difficult for those who follow Jesus. It's not that he wants to cause turmoil and strife, but the way of Jesus is vastly different than the rest of the world. It is distinctly countercultural. Jesus says that he came not to bring peace, but a sword, and to set a household against itself, "a man against his father, and a daughter against her mother, and a daughter-in-law against her mother-in-law" (Matt 10:35).

When you were converted, you ceased to be who you used to be, and as you put off the old and put on the new and are gradually transformed and conformed into the image of Christ, you become more like the you will be at the end of time. It's confusing, I know, but a lack of understanding does not make it untrue. When the Holy Spirit regenerates your heart and you cry out to God for rescue, the work is already done on your behalf.

And God transfers you out of a kingdom of darkness and into citizenship in light. By the work of God, you are a part of a new community consisting of a regenerated humanity, one that more

Building Up the Body (Part II)

closely resembles what God intended for humanity from the time of the garden of Eden. This new humanity is bonded through the blood of Jesus rather than the blood of your ancestry. God welcomes you into his family and calls you a son or daughter in Christ and that comes will everything you think it would. It secures a future, it makes you part of the inheritance, it connects you with other members of the family who don't look or talk like you. Your life is tied up with that of Christ because you are part of his family.

And this family has a purpose: to testify to the glory of God.

It's been God's purpose for humanity from the beginning, right? God created the universe and then he revealed himself because he wants to be known and worshiped. The whole purpose of creation and the Bible hasn't changed. Over the centuries, the goal remains the same: bring glory to God. And the command Jesus gives to the disciples between his resurrection and his ascension reflects that: "Go therefore and make disciples of all nations, baptizing them in the name of the Father and of the Son and of the Holy Spirit, teaching them to observe all that I have commanded you" (Matt 28:19–20). This is both what we do as individuals to glorify him and how we, the church, spread God's fame and glory over the earth. Both sides of that coin matter.

What do we do to glorify God? The outcome of gospel is disciples that make disciples. In other words, every disciple is a disciple-maker in training. The process of making a disciple is straightforward. We're given an example of what that looks like through the life of Jesus. Robert Coleman's *The Master's Plan of Evangelism* provides a brilliant explanation of what evangelism and discipleship look like.

> Jesus intended for the disciples to produce his likeness in and through the church being gathered out of the world. Thus his ministry in the Spirit would be duplicated manyfold by his ministry in the lives of his disciples. Through them and others like them it would continue to expand in and ever-enlarging circumference until the

The Blueprint of Grace

multitudes might know in a similar way the opportunity that they had known with the Master.[1]

Practically, it looks like living life with people as Jesus did; leading and teaching and mentoring and guiding those who are far from God into an understanding what a relationship with him is about. Then, when they are ready to stand up and publicly declare themselves sinners in need of salvation and that their debt to sin was paid by Jesus, we baptize them as a demonstration they believe Jesus is the Son of God, that he died to restore our relationship with God the Father, that God raised him from the dead on the third day, that he ascended to heaven but is coming back someday to reign over all the earth for eternity, and that this reality is life-changing. And we don't leave them there. That's where last chapter comes in. We as a church gather around new believers and help them to understand what regeneration means and how that impacts the rest of their lives. The church steps into the gap to teach young converts to carry forward everything that Jesus taught.

That's what the Great Commission is all about. Making disciples who can and will become reproducing disciples.

How does this glorify God? His people, plural—the entirety of this new gospel-formed family—cover the earth with demonstrations and proclamations of his glory, make known who he is, and lead others into this very same relationship that brought us into the family. Have you ever considered that one of the purposes of any family is to increase the size of the family? God gave mankind the mandate to be fruitful and multiply in order to cover and subdue the earth. Every family, working in alignment with God's plan for it, grows. Why would God's chosen family through Christ look any different? If a family unit naturally grows through reproduction, shouldn't God's family reproduce and grow as well?

One of the constants and themes of the Bible is that if God ordains a structure, it never goes away. In Genesis 1, the triune God establishes the family as his method of representation on the earth in his stead. That structure has never gone away. As the

---

1. Coleman, *Master Plan of Evangelism*, 99.

Building Up the Body (Part II)

Israelites prepare to enter into the promised land, God tells them that his commandments are to be on their hearts and taught to their children and children's children. In every situation, traveling or at home, parents are to model holiness to their progeny. The older generation must teach the younger generation what God has done. It's a cycle that never goes away and God intends the family to serve as the primary unit for this instruction.

When the Israelites cross the Jordan River and enter into the promised land for the first time, before God conquers their enemies before them, Joshua gives a command"

> Pass on before the ark of the LORD your God into the midst of the Jordan, and take up each of you a stone upon his shoulder, according to the number of the tribes of the people of Israel, that this may be a sign among you. When your children ask in time to come, 'What do those stones mean to you?' then you shall tell them that the waters of the Jordan were cut off before the ark of the covenant of the LORD. When it passed over the Jordan, the waters of the Jordan were cut off. So these stones shall be to the people of Israel a memorial forever. (Josh 4:5–7)

One generation must prepare the next for the task of carrying the ministry forward.

No one else is going to proclaim the goodness of God except those who have experienced the goodness of God. Who else would? And so we grow together as Christians. We each share our experiences. We encourage one another to grow in our understanding of God's work. We remind each other of the work God has done through Christ on our behalf. We commit to pray for one another in our hardships and struggles. We celebrate victories over sin and times when God provided when no other provision would suffice. We correct each other and confess to one another when it's necessary, when our lives don't reflect what we believe to be true about the gospel.

We do all of that so that our lives become more and more like Christ, both inside the community of the church and outside of it.

The Blueprint of Grace

We engage in all of these activities in the public square, too. We don't hide what God is doing inside the walls of the church. We talk about him and his work in our lives when we're conversing with people at our workplace. We ask the parents of our child's classmates how we can be praying for them. We check in with the principal about what needs teachers have so that we might be able to meet them. We show up to the sporting event keeping a close watch on our language and behavior. We live out, in part, as Francis of Assisi is reputed to have said: "Preach the gospel at all times, and if necessary use words." We live above reproach, winsomely caring for others and speaking the truth with them in love.

It's not the job of the few, but the many. God gave the church the assignment to multiply itself, which means he gave every Christian, the entire body of believers—each individual—a role in that process. No Christian is exempt from growing and, likewise, no Christian is exempt from participating in God's redemptive work in the world. This job was given to us by the one who saved us in the first place, for his glory.

I can't remember where I first came across or heard this idea, but your salvation is not just about you. Sure, you receive the benefit of eternity with God, but God gets the glory for displaying his goodness toward you. Secondarily, through having your eternity secured by Christ, the people in your life get a front row seat to God working in your life, which means that your salvation is for them too. They can see, tangibly, that the gospel changed your life and so they get to vicariously experience the freedom you have in Christ, a freedom to pour yourself out for others because you don't have to concern yourself with what is going to happen to you.

Because nobody but a child of God can explain what that's like.

And being a child of God means having a glorious future.

11

The Future Glory of the Church and You

> For you have died, and your life is hidden with Christ in God. When Christ who is your life appears, then you also will appear with him in glory.
>
> —Colossians 3:3–4

We've been on this journey for a while.

Whether you've been a Christian for sixty years or sixty seconds, the end seems both near and far. At any moment, God could call you home to him, but then again your life could last for decades longer than it has already.

My goal in writing this book has been to help you see that the path God set you on when he saved you is one that ends in heaven. He has promised to bring you to him through Christ and so God provides a map for the journey, complete with turn-by-turn advice and guidance in the Bible. It is a trek full of highs and lows and twists and turns. There will be easy days and there will be hard days, and so he gives you a family, the church, to encourage you, strengthen you, prepare you, and walk beside you along the way.

All of it comes because God has saved you. When he saves you, he restores things to their intended working order. You are set free from the burden of trying to live the perfect life. It's a life you cannot possibly succeed in. As hard as that is to hear, in your heart of hearts you probably, and possibly begrudgingly, know it to be true. But in Christ you are unburdened from the weight of your sin. Your pursuit of God is freed up from wondering whether or not you will measure up in the end. "For you have died, and your life is hidden with Christ in God" (Col 3:3).

This beautiful truth leads us to the end—not just of the book, but of all things.

> "When Christ who is your life appears, then you also will appear with him in glory" (Col 3:4)

That sounds nice, but what does that even mean?

It means that your future is far brighter than you can imagine. Reality can be hard to wrap your head around, but other places in the Bible give shape to what it means for you to appear with Christ in glory.

> And I heard a loud voice from the throne saying, "Behold, the dwelling place of God is with man. He will dwell with them, and they will be his people, and God himself will be with them as their God. He will wipe away every tear from their eyes, and death shall be no more, neither shall there be mourning, nor crying, nor pain anymore, for the former things have passed away." And he who was seated on the throne said, "Behold, I am making all things new." Also he said, "Write this down, for these words are trustworthy and true." And he said to me, "It is done! I am the Alpha and the Omega, the beginning and the end. To the thirsty I will give from the spring of the water of life without payment. The one who conquers will have this heritage, and I will be his God and he will be my son." (Rev 21:3–7)

The Future Glory of the Church and You

At the end of all things, those who have been redeemed by the blood of the Lamb spend eternity in the presence of God. There is a return to a state of peace between God and mankind, a return to a garden:

> Then the angel showed me the river of the water of life, bright as crystal, flowing from the throne of God and of the Lamb through the middle of the street of the city; also, on either side of the river, the tree of life with its twelve kinds of fruit, yielding its fruit each month. The leaves of the tree were for the healing of the nations. No longer will there be anything accursed, but the throne of God and of the Lamb will be in it, and his servants will worship him. They will see his face, and his name will be on their foreheads. And night will be no more. They will need no light of lamp or sun, for the Lord God will be their light, and they will reign forever and ever. (Rev 22:1–5)

What you do about that between now and then is the rest of your life. I can tell you that what God desires from you is still the same as it has always been.

From before the beginning of time, God's plan for you as a person involved in the past, involves presently, and will always involve in perpetuity submitting yourself to him because he knows you best. He knows what makes you smile. He knows what gives you pause. He knows your insecurities. He knows your faults and flaws. He knows your strengths and dreams. He knows everything about you. He know when you're going to step off the path. He knows when you will be distracted by things and desires that are not from him. He knows what you have faced in your adolescence, in your past choices, and knows exactly what you will face in your job, in your family, in your heart, in your church, and in your relationships in the future, both near and far.

And, wonder of wonders, he loves you.

Through all of the highs and lows you will see in your lifetime, God never deserts you. You may feel like he is not there, as

The Blueprint of Grace

though you are alone. You may find yourself in some of the hard moments questioning the Father's dedication to you.

Don't. Please, don't.

The Creator of the universe, the Designer and Power behind everything that has ever been created, the triune God, in the form of Father, Son, and Spirit, loves you. He will never leave nor forsake you. And he demonstrated that love by coming to earth to buy you back from yourself.

God has promised you something beyond imagining, beyond any hope you could hold out for yourself by your own effort. He who began this good work in you will bring it to completion on the day of Christ Jesus, our Lord.

Amen.

Conclusion
An Invitation

So, the question now becomes: What are you going to do about it?

Let me put all of this together in an illustration that I think will be helpful.

The process of sanctification is a bit like a home remodeling television reality show. It begins with recognizing that you're in need of a major remodel. Just like all of these remodeling shows, there is a client—in this case you—and an architect—that's God.

The client hires the Architect, who looks around at the current space, taking note of the needs and wants of the client. The Architect then heads off to design the renovation and produces blueprints that give a glimpse of how the final product will fit what they call "the brief," the information given to shape what goes into the house. The Architect arrives at the job site, plans in hand, and casts a vision to the client about what it could be. Typically what the architect designs fits better than owner realizes or can see, but that realization rarely plays out until the end, when the final reveal happens and the architect is praised for going above and beyond expectation.

But what makes the show isn't the design process. It is not the vision of the architect, contractor, builder, owner, or whoever drew up the plans. While it is breathtaking when someone looks at a house, visualizes what *could* be based on the bare bones, then almost magically reconfigures the space to inject new vitality, the

The Blueprint of Grace

truly compelling aspect of this type of show is the tearing down and rebuilding.

If you're a fan of the genre, you probably know the stages by heart: demolition, snags, progress, and final reveal.

The producers decide to show bits and pieces of the demolition. There are sledge hammers and jackhammers and reciprocating saws ripping the interior to shreds. Sometimes they bring in heavy equipment like trackhoes to raze a section that needs to be rebuilt or removed. You can almost make a game out of what they will show in this phase because the shows really are all the same, yet still oddly compelling.

But there is always a catch, a fly in the ointment, an unforeseen problem, some detail that was either unaccounted for or overlooked that threatens to derail the project almost before it gets off the ground or send the budget spiraling due to the cost of fixing said flaw. The moment comes when they are explaining the problem to the homeowner and your stomach mimics their crestfallen expression, sinking as both you and they realize just how significant and critical it is to fix. For some, it's a minor speed bump, but occasionally the devastation of what that means for the project really hits home. The showrunners want you to feel the feels. They show you the fear and anxiety expressed on faces, in tremulous voices, through word choices like "major" and "doubt" and "setback" and "expensive." They want you to despair, so they dangle the scenario in front of you, and, doggone it, I swallow it hook, line, and sinker because *I* want this project to get done on time and on budget. How could anyone not want that?

But regardless of how bad the situation may appear, it's not the end of the world. It's like the professional wrestler who kicks out of a pin attempt at two-and-a-half, a split second before the referee slaps the mat a third time. Invariably, the issue is addressed. Costly? Yes. Time-consuming? Absolutely. Insurmountable? Nope.

This is the phoenix-rising moment. From the ashes of death and despair, the project springs back to life and confidence builds once again. I have yet to watch one of these shows and see the renovator give up and pack it in. Have you? There's a dogged

Conclusion

determination to finish and to do it well and to do whatever can be done to keep things on track and on plan and on budget. If you've ever watched one of these shows, you've seen it: there's a "mad dash to the finish line" and "amazing effort and hard work" and "people working around the clock."

And then it's over.

The next shot you see is of the completed project. Cameras pan around exteriors and interiors to give some context and scope. Before and after views highlight what is often radical renewal. The outcome displays far more than a fresh coat of paint; it's more transformation than reformation. What once existed can be seen by the critical eye, but the old can be hard to see due to the drastic changes; the old bones and structure still exist, but the dramatic alterations have created something altogether new.

The results speak for themselves: smiles, relief, grins, celebrations, laughter, occasionally tears of joy, and the like. The build finally realized and completed, the involved parties—the builders, the architects, the designers, and the clients—gather to recall the journey; highs and lows, ups and downs.

God wants to remodel your life. He wants to help you tear out the harmful aspects of your life and the parts that lead you away from him. He wants you to build your life around what he says in his Word and, knowing you will face setbacks and hardships and challenges, he wants you to continue to trust in his provision for you. Since he knows what you need is more than just words, he embodies those words through his chosen family of believers to support and encourage you as you grow in your knowledge of his will and purpose. Further still, he wants to use your life as a living testimony to what he is able to do when someone cedes control over to him. In the end, when you do so, you will see a future more glorious than anything you have ever seen before, an eternity spent in the joy of the Master.

Will you let the Architect show you a blueprint of what he can do with your life?

Will you allow him to lead you through the process of remodeling your heart and life?

The Blueprint of Grace

Will you let him take you to the glorious future he has promised?

It will take hard work. It will be painful. It will at times feel hopeless.

But the end result, oh! The end result is nothing short of glory.

If you're ready, the Architect has the plan laid out for you. He's just waiting for you to ask him to start the project.

Will you?

Bibliography

"Baptist Faith and Message, 2000." Southern Baptist Convention. https://bfm.sbc.net/bfm2000/.

Begg, Alistair. "Spurgeon Lectures. Part 1." Lecture presented for Spurgeon Lectures on Biblical Preaching, Midwestern Baptist Theological Seminary, Kansas City, Missouri, October 2016.

Coleman, Robert. *The Master Plan of Evangelism*. Grand Rapids: Revell, 1993.

Crabb, Lawrence J., Don Hudson, and Al Andrews. *The Silence of Adam: Becoming Men of Courage in a World of Chaos*. Grand Rapids: Zondervan, 1995.

"Declaration of Independence: A Transcription." National Archives and Records Administration. https://www.archives.gov/founding-docs/declaration-transcript.

Frame, John M. "Divine Revelation: God Making Himself Known." The Gospel Coalition. https://www.thegospelcoalition.org/essay/divine-revelation-god-making-known/.

Garner, David. "The Holy Spirit: Agent of Salvation." The Gospel Coalition. https://www.thegospelcoalition.org/essay/the-holy-spirit-agent-of-salvation/.

Lewis, C. S. *Mere Christianity: Comprising the Case for Christianity, Christian Behaviour, and Beyond Personality*. New York: HarperCollins, 1998.

Ortlund, Dane. *Gentle and Lowly*. Wheaton, IL: Crossway, 2020.

Piper, John. "The Rebellion of Nudity and the Meaning of Clothing." Desiring God, April 24, 2008. https://www.desiringgod.org/articles/the-rebellion-of-nudity-and-the-meaning-of-clothing.

———. "We Will Never Outgrow the Gospel." Desiring God, February 22, 2019. https://www.desiringgod.org/messages/receive-with-meekness-the-implanted-word/excerpts/we-will-never-outgrow-the-gospel.

———. "What Does It Mean to Be Made in God's Image?" Ask Pastor John, Desiring God, August 19, 2013. https://www.desiringgod.org/interviews/what-does-it-mean-to-be-made-in-gods-image.

Bibliography

Saad, Lydia. "Record Few Americans Believe Bible Is Literal Word of God." Gallup, May 15, 2017. https://news.gallup.com/poll/210704/record-few-americans-believe-bible-literal-word-god.aspx.

Tozer, A. W., and James L. Snyder. *Delighting in God*. Minneapolis: Bethany House, 2015.

Westminster Shorter Catechism. Puritan Reformed Theological Seminary. https://prts.edu/wp-content/uploads/2016/12/Shorter_Catechism.pdf.

www.ingramcontent.com/pod-product-compliance
Lightning Source LLC
Chambersburg PA
CBHW060405090426
42734CB00011B/2266